FROM PAINTED SCROLLS TO ANIME:

LITERATURE
AND THE
ARTS OF JAPAN

Titles in the series include:

LUCENT LIBRARY *of* HISTORICAL ERAS

From Painted Scrolls to Anime:

Literature and the Arts of Japan

PATTY J. RULAND

LUCENT BOOKS
A part of Gale, Cengage Learning

GALE
CENGAGE Learning

Detroit • New York • San Francisco • New Haven, Conn • Waterville, Maine • London

© 2008 Gale, Cengage Learning

For more information, contact
Lucent Books
27500 Drake Rd.
Farmington Hills, MI 48331-3535
Or you can visit our Internet site at gale.cengage.com

LIBRARY OF CONGRESS CATALOGING-IN-PUBLICATION DATA
Ruland, Patty J.
From Painted Scrolls to Anime: Literature and the Arts of Japan / by Patty J. Ruland.
p. cm. -- (Lucent library of historical eras. Twentieth-century Japan)
Includes bibliographical references and index.
ISBN 978-1-4205-0026-4 (hardcover)
1. Arts--Japan--Juvenile literature. I. Title.
NX584.A1R85 2008
700.952--dc22
2007038127

ISBN-10: 1-4205-0026-0

Printed in the United States of America
2 3 4 5 6 7 12 11 10 09 08

Contents

Foreword

Looking back from the vantage point of the present, history can be viewed as a myriad of intertwining roads paved by human events. Some paths stand out—broad highways whose mileposts, even from a distance of centuries, are clear. The events that propelled the rise to power of Germany's Third Reich, its role in World War II, and its eventual demise, for example, are well defined and documented.

Other roads are less distinct, their route sometimes hidden from view. Modern legislatures may have developed from old tribal councils, for example, but the links between them are indistinct in places, open to discussion and interpretation.

The architecture of civilization—law, religion, art, science, and government—as well as the more everyday aspects of our culture—what we eat, what we wear—all developed along the historical roads and byways. In that progression can be traced every facet of modern life.

A broad look back along these roads reveals that many paths—though of vastly different character—seem to converge at a few critical junctions. These intersections are those great historical eras that echo over the long, steady course of human history, extending beyond the past and into the present.

These epic periods of time are the focus of Historical Eras. They shine through the mists of history like beacons, illuminated by a burst of creativity that propels events forward—so bright that we, from thousands of years away, can clearly see the chain of events leading to the present.

Each Historical Eras consists of a set of books that highlight various aspects of these major eras. For example, the Elizabethan England library features volumes on Queen Elizabeth I and her court, Elizabethan theater, the great playwrights, and everyday life in Elizabethan London.

The mini-library approach allows for the division of each era into its most significant and most interesting parts and the exploration of those parts in depth. Also, social and cultural trends as well as illustrative documents and eyewitness accounts can be prominently featured in individual volumes.

Historical Eras present a wealth of information to young readers. The lively narrative, fully documented primary and secondary source quotations, maps, photographs, sidebars, and annotated bibliographies serve as launching points for class discussion and further research.

In studying the great historical eras, students also develop a better understanding of our own times. What we learn from the past and how we apply it in the present may shape the future and may determine whether our era will be a guiding light to those traveling future roads.

Timeline

◆

1898 The Japanese architectural preservation movement begins.

1911 Raicho Hiratsuka helps start Japan's feminist movement by creating the women's literary magazine *Seito*.

1913 Takarazuka Revue Company, an all-women kabuki group, is established.

1918 The Japanese Creative Print Society establishes the *sosaku hanga* woodblock printmaking movement.

1922 The Imperial Hotel, designed by Frank Lloyd Wright, opens in Tokyo.

1946–74 The manga *Sazae-san* follows the story of one family's life after World War II.

1950 Kurosawa Akira's film *Rashomon* is released.

1963 Japanese artist Ono Yoko publishes *Grapefruit*.

1969 Kawabata Yasunari becomes the first Japanese author to win the Nobel Prize in Literature.

1972 The antiwar manga *Barefoot Gen* is first published.

1986 Japan's first hip-hop club opens.

1988 Yoshimoto Banana publishes her first book, *Kitchen*.

1989 Filmmaker Kurosawa Akira receives an honorary U.S. Academy Award for his influence on global cinema.

1994   Kansai International Airport opens. Japanese writer Oe Kenzaburo wins the Nobel Prize in Literature.

1997   The anime film *Mononoke-hime* wins the Japanese Academy Award for Best Film.

2004   The film *The Grudge* becomes one of the most popular works of J-horror in the United States.

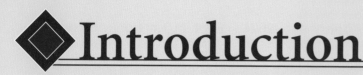
CREATING A UNIQUE CULTURE

Throughout history, Japan has been a cultural borrower. Its written language is adapted from Chinese characters. Its religion incorporates elements of Confucianism from China and Buddhism from India. Japan adopted Western political and military ideas as it modernized in the late nineteenth and early twentieth centuries. In each circumstance, Japan used cultural borrowing to adapt to global influences while maintaining its own identity. It took these outside elements and changed them to suit the Japanese way of life.

Japan has been a cultural lender as well. As professor Dr. M. Lal Goel explains,

> One popular stereotype is that the Japanese have been nothing more than borrowers and imitators. The truth is quite the contrary. Japan has developed in many independent ways. ...[T]he sliding paper paneled walls...the small manicured rock gardens which are copied the world over; the Zen method of meditation; distinctive cuisine and esthetic presentation; Kabuki and Noh Drama Theater; a sense of beauty and attention to detail unparalleled anywhere.[1]

In short, Japan has exported as much of its culture as it has imported. Beyond the familiar tatami mats and hibachi barbecues, Japan has made significant innovations in literature, fine art, architecture, theater, and cinema. In each instance, Japan has acted as a leader and not just a follower.

In literature, for example, Japan is credited with the creation of the world's first novel, *The Tale of Genji*, by Lady Murasaki. Written in the eleventh century, *The Tale of Genji* continues to inspire artists in the literary, visual, dramatic, and cinematic arts.

Japanese printmakers were among the world's first graphic artists to mass-produce ads and posters. Their eighteenth- and nineteenth-century woodblock prints drew customers to tea rooms, restaurants, and theaters. In addition, these prints inspired Western artists, such as Auguste Renoir and Vincent van Gogh. Japan's global influence on the visual arts continues today with the genres of manga and anime.

Japanese architects aspire to create harmony between nature and modern buildings. Their indoor gardens have inspired similar creations in urban settings around the world. Japan is home to one of the world's architectural marvels, Kansai International Airport. The airport, built on a human-made island in Osaka Bay, is an engineering and architectural wonder.

Japanese citizens were among the world's first advocates for architectural preservation, pushing for protective laws even before World War II. Their efforts inspired a national historic preservation movement and paved the way for similar movements around the world.

Likewise, Japanese filmmakers have inspired their counterparts around the world. Films by Kurosawa Akira, for example, directly influenced American movies such as *The Magnificent Seven* and *Star Wars*. In recent years, Japanese horror films, such as *The Ring* and *The Grudge*, have achieved international success as a unique genre known as J-horror.

All of Japan's arts, whether adapted through cultural borrowing or shared through cultural lending, illustrate Japan's unique character. This unique character is known as the Japanese aesthetic. This aesthetic includes an appreciation for nature and, in visual media, the use of clean lines and geometric shapes—what some call "an elegant simplicity."[2]

Against this backdrop, Japanese artists both adhered to tradition and courted change. With each passing decade, artists altered each art form, until major changes took hold. In doing so, they have sought to create a balance between tradition and change. It is through this lens that much of contemporary Japanese culture can be viewed: a unique combination of tradition and modernity. Writer Tanizaki Junichiro, for example, made a name for himself by recasting the traditional story of *The Tale of Genji* with more modern characters, such as a waitress and an engineer. Twentieth-century printmakers returned to eighteenth-century designs and production methods in reviving traditional Japanese woodblock printing. Traditional stories of samurai inspired generations of modern Japanese filmmakers, including Kurosawa Akira, as well as countless manga and anime artists, such as *Samurai Champloo* creator Watanabe Shinichiro.

Contact with Western culture challenged the Japanese aesthetic. Some artists remained true to Japanese tradition. Others abandoned tradition in favor of Western ideas. Many artists sought to combine the two influences. Writer Raicho Hiratsuka worked to incorporate the Western concept of women's rights into Japanese society. In Tanizaki Junichiro's novel *Naomi*, he presents the ideal woman as a Westernized movie star. Visual artists, such as Ono Yoko and Morimura Yasumasa, incorporated Western images into their work. The manga *Black Jack* resembled an American Western.

Throughout the twentieth century, Japanese artists in a variety of mediums were able to synthesize Japanese and Western concepts to create a distinctive Japanese cultural tradition. In this way, Japanese artists deserve credit for demonstrating the fact that Japan has been a center of cultural exchange for quite some time. These artists deserve credit, too, for illustrating how traditional and modern values can co-exist. The artists' ability to blend tradition and modernity shows that the two forces can work together. By working together, these forces create an art and culture unlike any other in the world—Japan's.

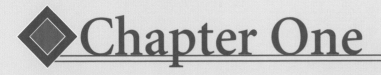

Chapter One

The Decorative and Fine Arts

Throughout history, Japanese artists have embraced tradition. Even in the face of modern forces, these artists have preserved what is uniquely Japanese while creating new art forms. In turn, these new art forms have had an important impact on art movements and artists around the world.

The acceptance of decorative art as fine art is one example of how Japanese artists have struck a balance between tradition and modern times. Decorative art is the creation of useful yet beautiful objects such as furniture, ceramics, and textiles. Fine art is the creation of objects such as paintings and sculptures that are simply pleasing to the eye. These pieces typically do not serve any functional or useful purpose.

Many art pieces now viewed as fine art were crafted hundreds of years ago as decorative art pieces. These pieces include woodblock prints, miniature carvings known as *netsuke*, and painted scrolls.

Artists used techniques and artistic principles unique to their culture to create these pieces for decoration or display.

Some modern Japanese artists have included these time-honored techniques and principles in their own pieces. Their work has influenced artists and art movements around the world. Many well-known Western artists latched onto Japanese decorative art and blended these traditional Japanese techniques into their own work. After 1945, this mix of Japanese traditional and modern art led to a strong artistic connection between Tokyo and New York.

In addition to its influence on Western artists, Japan has produced artists who have changed the art world, such as Ono Yoko and Morimura Yasumasa. Both Ono and Morimura illustrate how Japanese artists successfully mix traditional artistic principles with modern forces. Their work continues to impact young artists around the world.

The Great Wave Off Kanagawa, which was created around 1831, is part of Katsushika Hokusai's renowned Thirty-six views of Mount Fuji series of prints.

The Japanese Tradition of Decorative Art

In modern Japan, much of what people consider fine art was created as decorative art. Woodblock prints, netsuke, and painted scrolls from past eras have all found new life as works of fine art. These decorative art pieces were first made popular and affordable in the seventeenth century. The acceptance of such traditional art in modern times shows the appreciation that artists and art lovers have for traditional Japanese culture and artistic principles.

Woodblock Prints: Dispatches from the Floating World

Japanese artists excelled in the art of woodblock printmaking. This decorative art form evolved from earlier forms of printing, including prehistoric stone etchings and ancient Chinese rubbings. Most historians, however, credit the Japanese with producing the world's first prints.

Woodblock prints were one of the world's first forms of mass media. First created in the mid- to late 1600s, they were made by printing ink onto paper using blocks of wood. Early prints were made from black outline blocks and colored in by hand. The images created in this way were not perfect; they had asymmetrical and uneven lines. This use of irregularity in art is a Japanese artistic principle still seen today.

Woodblock prints were inexpensive to produce because the same block could be used to make many prints. Unlike other forms of Japanese art, people of almost any lifestyle could afford a woodblock print, which cost about the same as a bowl of noodles. The art form became extremely popular. Some woodblock print artists were quite prolific, which accommodated the extreme demand for their work. Artist Utagawa Kunisada, for example, designed fifty thousand prints.

Around the time that woodblock prints were becoming popular, entertainment districts called *ukiyo,* or "the floating world," developed in Japan's larger cities, such as Kyoto and Osaka. The floating world referred to the idea that life is fleeting, so people should enjoy themselves. Because they could be mass-produced, woodblock prints were used to advertise the amusements available in the ukiyo. These prints were called *ukiyo-e,* or "pictures of the floating world."

Without the lively ukiyo entertainment districts, ukiyo-e may not have endured. These woodblock prints showcased an entire subculture—the popular counterculture of the time. Subgenres of the art form included comical folk paintings, prints showing foreign people and objects, and prints portraying actors of Kabuki theater. Ukiyo-e was the first form of sensationalism—the use of shocking and disturbing imagery to grab people's attention. Artists began to use woodblock prints to express supernatural and violent scenes. These images were very different from the peace and cooperation most Japanese strove for in their daily lives. Balancing opposing forces in this way, however, is another artistic principle evident in Japanese art. As John Reeve observed, "Many writers have reflected upon what appears to be a duality in Japanese culture, between the serene [peaceful] and the turbulent."[3] Although appearing only occasionally in the decorative ukiyo-e arts, provocative imagery grew to dominate and define modern art.

Netsuke: Useful Decoration

Netsuke is another Japanese decorative art form now considered fine art. Netsuke first appeared in the early 1600s. They were small, decorative containers usually carved from ivory. Using natural objects such as ivory is another Japanese artistic principle.

Netsuke were no more than 3 inches (7.5 cm) long. Because the traditional kimono, or robe, did not have pockets, men carried their personal items—such as tobacco and pipes—in a pouch that hung from the sash about their waist. The netsuke secured the pouch to the sash. Although useful, netsuke had to be attractive, too. As one scholar noted, "To be a

鳥居清満画

New Prints and Creative Prints

The early twentieth century saw a revival in woodblock printmaking. Two movements, *shin hanga* (new prints) and *sosaku hanga* (creative prints), formed to meet the demand that had arisen in the United States for more authentic prints. Japanese shin hanga artists emulated the work of European impressionists, who had in their day tried to imitate the work of traditional ukiyo-e woodblock printmakers.

Shin hanga featured traditional subjects, such as landscapes and beautiful women, infused with Western light effects and moods. Publisher Watanabe Shozaburo founded the new print movement. New prints were produced the old-fashioned way: artists designed woodblock images and craftspeople did the actual carving and printing. Artists Ito Shinsui and Kawase Hasui were named Living Na-

Traditional woodblock print illustrating the gate of the Itsukushima Shrine

tional Treasures by the Japanese government for their shin hanga designs.

Sosaku hanga printmakers favored artistry over craftsmanship, with individual creativity held as the highest ideal. The Japanese Creative Print Society founded the movement in 1918. In contrast to new print artists, creative print artists were involved at every stage of the printmaking process. Sosaku hanga was not as commercially successful as shin hanga, but it was historically important because its artists embraced traditional Japanese artistic techniques and principles.

This woodblock print from the 1870s shows a woman wearing a silk kimono, obi, and wooden sandals.

good netsuke, an object had to be compact in shape and size, durable, with a smooth surface, and of course, preferably visually pleasing and decorative."[4]

At the time, the lower classes could not wear jewelry or clothing that showed

Netsuke, like this one made around 1870, were valued for both their artistic and practical purposes.

signs of wealth. This rule did not apply to netsuke, however. After all, they were not clothing or jewelry. Therefore, people of lower classes embraced the more elaborate designs. Flowers, animals, and characters from mythology were popular subjects for netsuke. As netsuke became more popular in the 1700s, netsuke artisans made their own signature styles, which were more ornate and complex than earlier designs.

Over time, netsuke became less popular until they became obsolete. There are several reasons for this. First, clothing changed from the traditional kimono to styles that were more modern. Because modern clothing often included pockets, netsuke were not needed. Second, the invention of cigarettes changed the need to carry tobacco and pipes. Today, netsuke are recognized for their beauty and artistry.

Painted Scrolls: From Portable to Priceless

One of Japan's greatest contributions to the art world is *kakemono,* or scroll painting. Kakemono refers to the creation of scrolls painted with characters (calligraphy), pictures, or both. A long piece of paper or cloth attached to a crossbar at either end serves as the canvas. A cord tied to the upper crossbar allows the piece to be hung on a wall.

Hanging scrolls came into use in China as early as the 600s. They were brought into Japan as part of the Buddhist tradition. For Buddhists, the scrolls were religious centerpieces. In Japan, the simplicity and beauty of the scrolls enhanced the atmosphere of tea ceremonies. During this time-honored ritual of entertaining guests with tea, a scroll would be hung at one end of the room. Kakemono soon took on a more artistic role.

Places of worship continued to display sacred scrolls, but pieces were found in estates, palaces, and teahouses as well. Subject matter for the scrolls included landscapes, birds, flowers, and other aspects of natural and rural life. Using nature for artistic inspiration is a Japanese artistic principle. Some scrolls included text in the form of letters or poems. Some Japanese artists created narrative scrolls, which unfolded from right to left and told stories through pictures.

Modernism to Avant-Garde

For thousands of years, Japanese artists honored tradition—what was uniquely Japanese. They embraced artistic principles such as using natural objects, gaining inspiration from nature, and balancing opposing forces. At the same time, they drew inspiration from other cultures, such as China and Korea. When Japan opened its doors to the West at the close of the Edo period (1600–1868), it set in motion unprecedented cultural exchange.

Soon after the door to Japanese trade opened, traditional Japanese decorative art became popular among Western consumers. The French coined the term *Japonisme* to refer to Japanese art. In the fine arts, many of the West's greatest artists, including Mary Cassatt and Vincent van Gogh, embraced Japonisme. In turn, Japanese artists adopted Western techniques. Over time, this mix of cultures affected art movements around the globe.

Japonisme

Japanese art influenced Western artists in significant ways. Western artists adopted the idea that art should be both functional and interesting to look at. They embraced the belief that art should be available to large numbers of people, just as woodblock prints and netsuke had been.

Some of the most influential artists of the West often used key elements of Japanese decorative arts in their own pieces. American painter and printmaker Mary Cassatt, for example, valued Japanese prints for their portrayal of women. Critic J.K. Huysmans praised Cassatt for

Traditional Japanese scrolls often depict religious themes, such as the Shaka Trinity.

"her clear-headed treatment of mothers and infants," whose intimate portraits were like the "pearls of Oriental sweetness"[5] depicted in Japanese art.

Artists in the West admired the simplicity of traditional Japanese woodblock prints. Woodblock-printing elements such as irregularity, strong outlines, and steep perspective can be found, for example, in the works of Vincent van Gogh. Similarly, Kubo Shumman's *A Party in the Four Seasons Restaurant by the Sumida River, Edo,* a woodblock print created in 1786, clearly influenced the use of diagonals and cropped space in Auguste Renoir's *Luncheon of the Boating Party.*

Japanese Modernism

Some Japanese artists adopted Western techniques, while others clung to tradition. For example, Italian instructors taught *yoga,* based on Western painting techniques, in Japanese art schools. *Nihonga* artists, on the other hand, held on to native Japanese themes and techniques. Teacher and tea master Kakuzo Okakura led the quest to preserve such Japanese artistic principles as using natural materials, turning to nature for inspiration, and embracing simplicity, imperfection, and asymmetry. In *The Book of Tea,* Kakuzo criticizes modern artists for "destroying the beautiful in life" and sacrificing the artistic for the scientific.[6]

Japanese artists who incorporated Western influences into their work did so partly in response to increasing governmental control of the arts. In 1907, the government began to dictate artistic styles and values. Artists rebelled by forming their own groups, especially after World War II. They explored Western art movements such as postimpressionism, cubism, and surrealism. Many artists broke with their cultural past and tradition in search of new forms of expression. This was the beginning of Japanese modernism.

The end of the Second World War marked a turning point for experimental Japanese artists, who pursued freedom of self-expression as a means of protest. Some of their artistic statements came about from necessity. For example, because there was a shortage of conventional materials after the war, some Japanese artists used whatever materials they could find. Most of these materials were not from nature, which was a distinct break with Japanese artistic principles. Shozo Shimamoto stuck pieces of newspaper together to make a canvas. Genpei Akasegawa created a series of wrapped objects, including a bottle, a suitcase, a jar, scissors, a hanger, a hammer, and a panel. Each piece was titled *Impounded Object.*

Many Japanese artists broke from the traditional Japanese artistic principle that nature should inspire art. Instead, they believed that art should reflect the real world, which at the time was filled with tragedy, injustice, and suffering. Most shared a common goal: to use their art to change society. Artists came together in groups to support each other and share ideas. This sharing led to important art movements.

The Total Art Movement

By the mid-twentieth century, experi-mental artists around the world wanted to unify many creative genres. The result was the total art movement. Artists started to feel confined by the notion that art should appear only on a canvas or inside a studio. They wanted to bring art to the streets and into nature. They created art that appealed to all five senses and with which the public could in-

French film director Jean Renoir (right) displays a reproduction of Luncheon of the Boating Party *by his father, Pierre-Auguste Renoir, in January 1942.*

teract. In addition, they created larger-than-life installations and pieces that could be mass-produced.

Traditional Japanese artistic principles contributed to the total art movement in significant ways. For instance, traditional Japanese art had always incorporated natural materials and had drawn inspiration from nature. Further, the idea of mass-producing art had roots in the Japanese woodblock prints. In addition, Japanese artists often worked to create a balance between opposing forces such as indoors/outdoors and art/nature.

The Avant-Garde Movement

The definition of *art* had been blown wide open by the total art movement. Now artists wanted to share their ideas. Japanese artists joined their Western counterparts in groups both at home and abroad. Artists in Tokyo and New York exchanged concepts, techniques, ideas, and inspiration. The intense artistic exchange between these cities—and the new and experimental art that came from it—has come to be known as avant-garde.

Seisakusha Kondankai (Artists Discussion Group) included painters, filmmakers, and writers. They combined art forms and schools of thought in an effort to guide young artists toward realism, or showing accurate representations of nature and real life in art. The group called *Gutai Bijutsu Kyokai* (Concrete Art Association) produced large-scale, interactive multimedia exhibits. The premier artist of the group was founder Jiro Yoshihara. He

was a painter who combined multimedia, performance, and theatrical art. The group focused on the process of art rather than the final product. This, too, was a traditional Japanese artistic principle. It influenced a major art movement called abstract expressionism, which encouraged the expression of attitudes and emotions through nontraditional means.

Japanese artists played a role in the spread of pop art, too. Pop art is short for popular art. Started in Britain in the 1950s, the pop art movement promoted what it called low art, or mass-produced gimmicks. Japanese pop art today draws upon traditional art such as woodblock prints.

Ono Yoko and Morimura Yasumasa

Japanese artists have influenced many art movements around the world. In their work, they embrace both Japanese artistic traditions and the experimental techniques unique to avant-garde art.

Two Japanese artists who have had a major impact on the art world are Ono Yoko and Morimura Yasumasa. Both strive to push the boundaries of the art world. In doing so, they continue the cultural exchange that has existed in Japanese art for centuries and constantly redefine what it means to be a Japanese artist.

Ono Yoko: The World's Most Famous Unknown Artist

Known to most of the world as the wife of musician John Lennon, Ono Yoko

The Japanese Aesthetic

The contributions of Japanese artists are often referred to as the Japanese aesthetic. Aesthetics has to do with what is considered beautiful or pleasing to the eye. The Japanese aesthetic is evident in Japan and throughout the West.

The features of the Japanese aesthetic are based on traditional artistic principles: the use of nature and natural materials, simplicity, imperfection and irregularity, and a balance of opposing ideas. The Japanese aesthetic encourages open spaces, or the idea that less is more. This idea is called minimalism. In addition, the Japanese aesthetic promotes integrating art into everyday life and emphasizing the process of creation and not simply the product.

A landscape print by Hiroshige (1797–1858), entitled The Snowstorm, depicts The Tama River in Musashi Province.

(more commonly known as Yoko Ono) is most recognizable as a media icon with long black hair and sunglasses. Lennon called his wife the "world's most famous unknown artist"[7] because his career clearly overshadowed hers, even though she had worked as an artist long before she met him.

Ono was born in Tokyo in 1933 to a well-to-do family. While attending college as the first female philosophy student at Gakushuin University in Tokyo in 1952, she became interested in the postwar Japanese avant-garde art move-ment. Soon, however, she left Japan to join her family, who had moved to New York. It did not take long for her to discover the thriving art community in lower Manhattan. She arrived at a time when non-Western cultures such as Japan's were inspiring new forms of artistic expression.

One group of artists that formed as a result of this move away from Western culture called themselves Fluxus. Fluxus artists mixed poetry, music, and visual arts. They embraced simplicity and open spaces. They valued the creative process over the end product. They balanced opposing forces such as playful/provocative and visionary/subversive. In addition, they used whatever materials were available. Many of these ideas reflected traditional Japanese artistic principles.

Ono became a member of Fluxus and exhibited her work in New York, London, and Tokyo. Her exhibits included poetry, film, and performance art. Over the years, she has continued to embrace Japanese artistic principles, such as simplicity, nature, and natural objects, in her work. For example, her first book, *Grapefruit*, was a work of poetry in the form of instructions to the reader—many having to do with nature. "Imagine the clouds dripping. Dig a hole in your garden to put them in," reads one of the entries, "Cloud Piece," written in 1963. *Grapefruit* greatly influenced the experimental art world and other artists, including Lennon. Just before his death in 1980, Lennon admitted that *Grapefruit* had inspired his most popular hit, "Imagine."

Ono continued to use nature and to balance opposing forces in her work. When she expanded *Grapefruit*'s instructions, for example, she included a recording of snow falling. Her goal was to mock the midcentury art scene, which she felt was obsessed with money and image.

In 2004, Ono exhibited Odyssey of a Cockroach, a statement against societal violence, including murder, domestic violence, and war. The work was composed of large-scale photographs and props that took up three floors in a building in London. The final section of the exhibit,

Yoko Ono with John Lennon at the London airport in 1971.

which included images of Europe during World War II, was interactive, allowing visitors to add their own messages.

Ono's art was mocked, scorned, and dismissed for much of her career. Now in her seventies, she is finally receiving recognition. Critic Peter Frank describes her as "one of the most daring, innovative and eccentric artist-performers of her time."[8]

Morimura Yasumasa: Master of Pun Art

A common objective of experimental art has been to make fun of the art world for being selective in its acceptance of artists and fine art. Morimura Yasumasa, one of the world's most popular contemporary artists, has distinguished himself as a master of parody. In parody, an artist imi-

Eisuke's Little Girl

The subject of the photo, Ono Yoko, is the great-granddaughter of billionaire banker Yasuda Zenjiro. Ono was born in 1933 at her great-grandfather's estate in Tokyo and attended by scores of servants. Her father, Eisuke, and mother, Isoko, were wealthy, too. What the posed, traditional portrait cannot reveal, however, are the struggles she experienced growing up in a country damaged by war. As a child, Ono fled Tokyo during a firebombing in World War II, only to be refused food by the poor in the countryside. She coaxed her brother, faltering due to hunger, to picture imaginary treats.

Ono remembers, "I asked him, 'What would you like to eat?' He said, 'Ice cream.' So I said, 'Imagine there is a lot of ice cream in a pail. Have as much as you want!' He got excited and looked so happy. We played this imaginary game every day and managed to survive through those difficult times from hunger."[1]

[1]Quoted in Roy H. Williams, "Eisuke's Little Girl," *The Monday Morning Memo*, October 27, 2003, http://www.monday-morningmemo.com/?ShowMe=This-Memo&MemID=1474(accessed March 10, 2007).

tates a style for comic effect or to ridicule. Morimura employs this technique to both honor and make fun of the traditional art world.

Morimura's art reflects a sense of *kazari*, or "ornament," in a unique and larger-than-life exhibit style. His work consists of images in which he superimposes his own face on the faces of famous figures in art, cinema, and history. Painting on his face instead of a canvas, he is known as the artist with a thousand faces.

Morimura has said his main goal is to be entertaining, but his puns go beyond fun. He uses them to make a political statement. In each category of parody, Morimura's art follows the traditional Japan-ese artistic principle of balancing opposing forces: "[This] male/female juxtaposition is just one of a number of oppositions in his work: traditional vs. modern, Western vs. Asian, and public vs. private,"[9] according to art critic Jeff Michael Hammond.

In 1985, Morimura recast Vincent van Gogh's face as his own for a collection of photographs, sculptures, videos, and print club machines. He called this exhibit Self-Portrait as Art History and traveled around the world with it. This series parodied the subjects and techniques of fine art masterpieces. Morimura's goal was to blur the lines between fine art and the rest of human self-expression.

Yoko Ono and John Lennon pose with a copy of Grapefruit, *Ono's book of "Instruction and Drawings," that was published in 1971.*

Morimura expanded this approach in 1996 in his Sickness unto Beauty—Self Portrait as Actress exhibit. In this exhibit, he replaced actresses' faces in classic movie scenes with his own. The installation resembled a movie theater and included billboards, a ticket booth, and a screening room.

In mocking film idols, Morimura spoke out against the popular definition of beauty. By impersonating Hollywood starlets, he intended to defend the unadorned, natural human appearance and imperfect self. For all the art and tricks, Morimura's true allegiance is to barefaced reality.

In another exhibit, called Yasumasa Morimura: Los Nuevos Caprichos, the artist placed his image within reconstructed prints by Spanish painter Francisco de Goya. The Goya originals, finished in 1799, depict greed and corruption in Spain. Because of their critical messages, they were hidden during the Spanish Inquisition. "Morimura may be working in a much more open climate today, but he obviously feels that Goya's themes are still relevant now," commented art critic Jeff Michael Hammond.[10]

In 2006, Morimura substituted his face in some of the world's most famous photographs, such as Lee Harvey Oswald being shot by Jack Ruby and a member of the Vietcong being executed in 1968. This exhibit, called Season of Passion, was pivotal in that Morimura began to portray male as well as female icons. In an interview, the artist explains why:

> There are two kinds of beings in the world: ones like Amaterasu [the Japanese Sun Goddess] and others like Susanoo [God of Storm and Sea]. Awful historic events in the 20th century were men's doing—I think, provoked by the Susanoo in them. For a long time, I produced works that embraced the values represented by Amaterasu, particularly with the 'Actress' series. And I see that the Japanese society has changed to accept and appreciate such values. While we accomplished that, we probably forgot about men, although masculine values led and created the 20th century.[11]

Traditional Japanese culture and artistic principles continue to influence artists and their work. These principles are evident in decorative art pieces that were created centuries ago and continue to permeate art in the present. They have stood the test of time because they speak to both artists and art lovers. When artists balance what is uniquely Japanese with the principles of other cultures, the result comes full circle to a basic Japanese artistic principle—balancing opposing forces by creating something that is both pleasing to the eye and thought provoking.

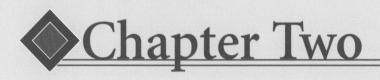

Chapter Two

Writing Modern Japan

Modern Japanese literature, much like Japanese art, includes a unique blend of traditional and modern. It reflects contemporary social change while including forms that have been used in Japan for centuries. The Tokugawa Era (1600–1868) witnessed the development of *mono no aware*, a concept that has come to define Japanese literature. Although difficult to translate directly into English, mono no aware roughly means "sensitivity to all things." Japanese literature expressed this sensitivity in its sympathetic understanding of nature and people's connection to it.

In the mid-nineteenth century, Japan was forced to open its ports to foreign trade. Doing so ended more than two centuries of self-imposed isolation and opened the door to Western ideas. During the Meiji period (1868–1912), these ideas gained wider acceptance and became incorporated into Japan's literary tradition. Literary artists soon developed a uniquely Japanese style that combined mono no aware and elements of Western culture.

Authors Kawabata Yasunari and Oe Kenzaburo gained international recognition for the traditional Japanese elements featured in their works. Others, such as Raicho Hiratsuka, Tanizaki Junichiro, and Yoshimoto Banana, drew attention to the changes in Japan—especially for women—brought by Western and modern influences. In more recent decades, the *manga*, or graphic novel, a twentieth-century adaptation of a seventeenth-century form, has become a multi-million-dollar international cultural export. While it is distinctly Japanese, manga—like the rest of modern Japanese literature—continues to gain a larger international following.

The Essence of Japan

Nature is a common theme in Japanese literature as it is in Japanese art. Such is the essence of mono no aware. Respect for the natural world can be traced throughout Japan's twentieth-century literature, from the early works of Kawabata Yasunari to the later works of Oe Kenzaburo, both of whom won Nobel Prizes. As Nobel Prize winners, these authors became international spokespeople for Japanese culture. Their writings serve as windows into the Japanese soul.

Of Nature and Human Feelings

Kawabata Yasunari (1899–1972) lived in the country with his grandfather before attending Tokyo Imperial University in the early 1920s. He helped found the magazine *Bungei Jidai* (Literary Age),

Kawabata Yasunari (far right) received the Nobel Prize for Literature on December 12, 1968, in Stockholm, Sweden.

which featured modern Japanese literature. Kawabata's first work of fiction, a short story titled "The Izu Dancer," was published in 1927. His novel *Yukiguni (Snow Country)*, published in 1937, made Kawabata one of Japan's most prominent authors. His body of work, according to the Nobel Foundation, made "the deepest impression in the author's native country and abroad."[12] Kawabata received the Nobel Prize in Literature in 1968 "for [his] narrative mastery which, with great sensibility, expresses the essence of the Japanese mind."[13]

Kawabata was the first Japanese writer to receive the Nobel Prize and the first Asian to win any Nobel Prize in more than fifty years. In his acceptance speech, Kawabata referred to the mono no aware concept that defined the Japanese aesthetic. He talked of "the snow, the moon, the blossoms, words expressive of the seasons as they move one into another, include in the Japanese tradition the beauty of mountains and rivers and grasses and trees, of all the myriad [countless] manifestations of nature, of human feelings as well."[14]

Kawabata paid tribute to the influence of Japanese religions in his work. He described a Zen Buddhist "universe of the spirit in which everything communicates freely with everything. ...[T]he emphasis is less upon reason and argument than upon intuition, immediate feeling. Enlightenment comes not from teaching but through the eye awakened inwardly."[15] This concept reflects another uniquely Japanese element in Kawabata's writing.

The novel *Yukiguni* makes extensive use of natural and religious imagery and themes. It tells the story of an affair between a middle-aged man named Shimamura and an aging geisha, or professionally trained female artist, named Komako. They conduct their affair at a hot springs resort west of the central mountains, where winters are silent, snow-covered, and bleak. According to scholar Ronny Green,

> Kawabata takes the reader away from the mundane world and into one covered with whiteness and purity. ... Snow covers all of the natural elements of the phenomenal world making it seem fantastic or dreamlike. In [Kawabata's] use of white there is a feeling of purity of the country and a stark separation is created between this pure land and the ordinary world the reader and characters have left.[16]

The snow-covered mountains become a sacred place where Kawabata's characters look inward and explore their lives and feelings. In doing so, they embody not only the essence of Zen Buddhism but also the concept of mono no aware.

Soul of a Storyteller

Oe Kenzaburo (1935–), another Japanese Nobel Prize winner, was born in the village of Ose-mura on the island of

Shikoku. Oe's birthplace has influenced his work and is the focus of the mono no aware in his writing.

Ose-mura cannot be found on a map. No one in Oe's family had ever left the village. In this remote, forested place, women were storytellers, keepers of legend and history of the region. During World War II, however, military education infiltrated every town, including remote locations such as Ose-mura. Countering this influence were the traditional stories that Oe heard from his grandmother and the Western literary classics that his mother gave to him, including *The Adventures of Huckleberry Finn* by Mark Twain. The effects of these works, he told biographers, "he will carry to the grave."[17]

After World War II, schools throughout Japan taught democratic principles. Oe "took democracy straight to his heart."[18] He left his village for Tokyo, seeking new opportunities that democracy afforded him. Oe enrolled at Tokyo University, where he studied the works of French and American authors. These authors helped shape Oe's emerging view of society and humanity.

Oe's career as a writer began in 1957. Many of his works focused on village and city life. His short story, "The Catch," published in 1957, and his first novel,

Bud-Nipping, Lamb Shooting, published in 1958, both told how war tore his village apart. In other works, Oe portrayed how the American presence affected life in Tokyo. His aim was to create a new form of literature that offered a "model for this contemporary age" based on his life in Ose-mura.[19]

The New Woman

In addition to reflecting their appreciation for nature, Japanese writers found they could use their works to discuss social issues. In some ways, this was an outgrowth of Japan's contact with Western ideas at the end of the nineteenth century. The reforms of the Meiji period, inspired by Western practices such as democracy, led to Western-inspired movements, including women's rights. The Meiji government passed laws that allowed girls and women access to public education and laws that established women's colleges. Women began to join the workforce. Many women worked outside the home during the years that Japan was at war. At the same time, however, the Japanese government continued to place many limits on the rights of women. A wife could not enter into a legal contract without her husband's permission. She could not share his estate after his death or retain custody of children after a divorce. Women could not join political organizations or hold public meetings. Yet out of this society came strong women writers with distinct voices who spoke for Japanese women and

The Beautiful Language of Birds

The birth of Oe's first son, Hikari, profoundly changed Oe's life and work. Hikari suffered a birth defect that left him disabled. The book *A Personal Matter* (1968) tells how Oe accepted Hikari into his life. In *My Deluged Soul (1973)*, Oe writes about a father who communicates through the songs of birds with a son who cannot speak. The story was based on Oe's experience with his own son. He described the incident in his 1994 Nobel acceptance speech:

> After I got married, the first child born to us was mentally handicapped. ... As a baby he responded only to the chirps of wild birds and never to human voices. One summer when he was six years old we were staying at our country cottage. He heard a pair of water rails warbling from the lake beyond a grove, and he said with the voice of a commentator on a recording of wild birds: "They are water rails." This was the first moment my son ever uttered human words. ... Birds were the originators that occasioned and mediated his composition of human music.[1]

[1]Oe Kenzaburo, "Japan, The Ambiguous, and Myself" (Nobel Lecture, December 7, 1994), ©The Nobel Foundation, 1994, *From Les Prix Nobel. The Nobel Prizes 1994*, Editor Tore Frängsmyr, [Nobel Foundation], Stockholm, 1995, http://nobelprize.org/nobel_prizes/literature/laureates/1994/oe-lecture.html (accessed July 9, 2007).

found a following around the world.

"I am the sun"— Feminism's Star

Raicho Hiratsuka (1886–1971) helped found the Japanese feminist movement. She established *Seitosha*, or the Blue Stocking Society, which published a magazine named *Seito*. The magazine was a forum for women's literary works and political ideas. It distinguished itself from other women's magazines of the time by calling for women's spiritual revolution.

Raicho was expected to get married and lead an uneventful life, but she chose a different path. She boycotted morals class because it stressed stereotypical female virtues. Raicho enrolled in Japan Women's College in 1903, when less than one percent of Japanese women pursued higher education. She studied Western philosophy and Japanese history, which inspired her work as a writer and as a women's rights activist.

In 1911, Raicho started a women's literary journal called Seito, which means "Blue Stocking." *Seito's* contributors wrote fiction and poetry and translated works of French and Russian writers. The journal eventually widened its scope to include social issues that affected women. In doing so, *Seito* became known as a "training school" for the so-called New Woman.

Raicho proved to be an artistic and political powerhouse who led her generation to a new feminist awareness. She wrote in a poem, "In the beginning, woman was truly the sun. An authentic person. Now she is the moon, a wan and sickly moon, dependent on another, reflecting another's brilliance."[20] Raicho invoked the image of a lost sun to inspire Japanese women to reclaim their sense of self-worth and creativity, and fulfill their human potential.

In addition to her literary efforts, Raicho campaigned for women's suffrage and workers' rights. Doing so secured her a place in history as both a literary figure and a social reformer.

The Father of Naomism

Tanizaki Junichiro (1886–1965) was a prolific writer whose career lasted through the reigns of three emperors. He won acclaim for his stories of urban life in Japan during the 1920s and 1930s. Tanizaki lived in Tokyo until the earthquake of 1923. Then he moved to the Kyoto-Osaka region, which was the setting of one of his most important novels, *The Makioka Sis-*

Formative Feminism

During the 1870s and 1880s, members of Japan's Freedom and People's Rights movement demanded rights for women. These were important years for Raicho Hiratsuka, who wrote "In The Beginning, Woman Was the Sun." The poem was a strong plea for equality:

The new woman; I am a new woman.
I seek, I strive each day to be that truly new woman I want to be.
In truth, that eternally new being is the sun.
I am the sun.

I seek; I strive each day to be the sun I want to be. . . .
The new woman today seeks neither beauty nor virtue.

She is simply crying out for strength, the strength to create this still unknown kingdom, the strength to fulfill her own hallowed [sacred] mission.[1]

[1]Quoted in Gen Kanai Weblog, "Poetry of Hiratsuka Raicho, Japanese Suffragette, 1911," http://www.kanai.net/weblog/archive/2001/01/20/15h18m29s (accessed July 8, 2007).

ters. Other influential works include *Naomi* and modern versions of *The Tale of Genji* (1941, 1954, and 1965). He received Japan's Imperial Prize in Literature in 1949.

Tanizaki's characters are often torn between two worlds, the East and the West, much as Japan was in the early twentieth century. Tanizaki's life reflects these competing cultures. As a resident of Tokyo, he was drawn to Western and modern influences. He lived in a Western-style house with his wife and child and studied Western literature at the university. Tanizaki's life changed significantly in the aftermath of the 1923 earthquake. The Kyoto-Osaka region to which he moved had a more traditional Eastern environment. There, Tanizaki grew to condemn Western influences.

Ironically, in turning to the past and Japanese tradition for inspiration, Tanizaki originated a modern cultural standard. His novel *Naomi*, published in 1924, gave rise to Naomism. A woman who was a Naomi wished to break free from tradition and live the life of the New Woman. Even the name, Naomi, is both Japanese and Western.

Naomi tells the story of a plain but prosperous engineer who falls in love with a 15-year-old waitress. He worships her and attempts to mold her into his ideal woman, a Westernized movie star. The plot resembles the Japanese classic *The Tale of Genji*, written in the eleventh century by a Japanese noblewoman. Many scholars consider *The Tale of Genji* to be the world's oldest novel. In the story,

a nobleman named Genji raises a young girl to become an empress. Tanizaki later wrote three versions of *The Tale of Genji* to express his growing preference for traditional values over modern ones.

Bananamania

Yoshimoto Banana (1964–   ) chose her pen name because she thought it was cute. She is known, however, for a series of serious and sensitive novels dealing with grief and tragedy. Yoshimoto became an international publishing sensation with the release of her first novel, *Kitchen*, in 1988. The story explores how a young woman, unmarried and living alone in the city, deals with the death of her mother.

Yoshimoto's father, a poet, book reviewer and activist, had quite an effect on his daughter. Yoshimoto Banana's work has earned her the reputation of being the voice of Generation X. Yoshimoto's portrayals of Japanese women gave rise to Bananamania, the term used to describe her popularity. Part of Yoshimoto's appeal is the story behind her literary success. A year before *Kitchen* was published, Yoshimoto was earning just under five hundred dollars a month as a waitress. Each day she would steal away to a coffee shop to work on her novel.

Not all of Yoshimoto's work is serious. She has engaged many critics as well as the public with her "cosmic kookiness and airy musings."[21] In keeping with the fruit motif in her name, two of her best-sellers were called *Pineapple Pudding*

Yoshimoto Banana's works have been published in more than 20 countries. In June 2004, she attended an international literature festival in Rome.

(1989) and *Fruit Basket* (1990). Indeed, many critics believe Yoshimoto Banana's works are as compelling as they are entertaining. According to one reviewer, some readers may find Yoshimoto's work to be "naïve, verging on amateurish."[22] This reviewer defends Yoshimoto by pointing out that readers must be familiar with Japanese culture to fully appreciate her works. As for Yoshimoto herself, she dreams of winning the Nobel Prize for Literature, of following the lead of other distinguished Japanese modern writers who introduced the world to the magic of Japanese literature.

Manga, Anyone? Manga, Everyone!

One of the most popular forms of Japanese literature is manga, or Japanese comic books. These comics are more like visual novels than American comic books. They are sometimes called graphic novels. Japanese of all ages and social classes read manga, which tells stories about many topics, including sports, comedy, and horror. Following World War II, manga helped peo-

Barefoot Voice of a Generation

Manga often depict important or complex issues. The manga *Hadashi no Gen* (*Barefoot Gen*), first published in the early 1970s, is one example. Created by artist Nakazawa Keiji, *Barefoot Gen* is an account of his family's experiences during World War II. Nakazawa was seven years old when the atomic bomb fell on his home city, Hiroshima.

> *Barefoot* Gen is known for its strong antiwar sentiment. Nakazawa explains, I named my main character 'Gen' in the hope that he would become a root or source of strength for a new generation, one that can tread the charred [burned] soil of Hiroshima barefoot, feel the earth beneath its feet, and have the strength to say "NO" to nuclear weapons. ... If you live through something like the A-bomb, you know that war is too horrible not to be avoided at all costs, regardless of the justifications offered for it.[1]

The manga illustrates the difficulties of life in wartime Japan, as well as the devastation and sickness caused by the atomic blast. According to Nakazawa, "[People] wanted to know what the war and the atomic bombing was really like. [*Barefoot Gen*] was the first time people had heard the truth."[2]

[1] Quoted in "Barefoot Gen," *Black Moon: Art, Anime, and Japanese Culture*, http://theblackmoon.com/BarefootGen/bomb.html (accessed July 8, 2007).
[2] Ibid.

ple understand Japan's new constitution. During the 1980s, it explained the workings and struggles of the Japanese economy. In recent years, manga has gained global popularity and developed into a multi-billion-dollar industry. Nonetheless, it is a unique art form that retains a cultural importance in Japan far exceeding that of comics in American culture.

Manga has achieved such great success because it is marketed to everyone. It tells stories of triumph and tragedy. Manga is a form of frank protest and of poetic celebration. For example, in 1994, the manga artist Hanawa was arrested for collecting guns. His work called *Doing Time* chronicles that experience in intimate detail. On the other end of the spectrum, Jiro Taniguchi's *The Man Who Walks* expresses an important aspect of

The Akira *manga debuted in Japan in 1982. Six years later, it became one of the first manga to be published in the United States.*

Captain Tsubasa is a well-known manga about Tsubasa Ozora, a boy who dreams of becoming the world's greatest soccer player.

the Japanese aesthetic: respect for nature. In this one-color (green) drawing, a wanderer takes in the sights—grass, shrubs, leaves, trees, and dappled light all around—in the middle of a bustling Japanese city.

Boy Manga

One type of manga is called boy manga. Due to a surge in popularity after World War II, boy manga became the best-selling sector of the market. Beginning in the 1940s and 1950s, boy manga focused on topics that society had typically associated with masculinity: competition, war, fighting, sports, technology, and physical humor. Boy manga featured aliens and androids—characters such as Ultraman, Eight Man and Muscleman, the Kamen Riders, and Power Rangers.

Tezuka Osamu's manga features Black

Jack, Two-Fisted Surgeon. It is a highly original version of the familiar "have gun, will travel" story line in many tales of the American Old West. With a scarred face and his scalpel drawn, Black Jack roams the land and performs graphically illustrated medical operations. Like his Old West counterparts, Jack is armed with strong principles but burdened by a mysterious past. In the tradition of most boy manga, these stories do not mask physical realities, whether bodily functions or fatal injuries.

Girl Manga

Manga is not limited to male heroes and male artists. Girl manga exists as well. Some critics fault these manga for promoting stereotypes of girls and women. In the manga of the early twentieth century, this was true. Girls and women featured in the manga of that era were depicted as passive and obedient. However, the picture is far more favorable in later manga. The female characters of modern girl manga, such as Princess Knight, are often strong, independent, and heroic.

The stars of girl manga include Hasegawa Machiko (1920–1992), Japan's first successful female comic artist. Hasegawa drew a daily family comic strip called *Sazae-san* from 1946 to 1974. *Sazae-san* followed three generations of the same family in their lives after World War II. After the war, manga gave teenage girls opportunities for exciting careers as cartoonists, just as it did for boys. In 1964, at age 16, Satonaka Machiko won a contest with the manga *Portrait of Pia*, a vampire story that launched her career and opened the field to other girls and women. Today, about 400 women artists create manga, with many enjoying enormous success. In 1993, Waki Yamato adapted *The Tale of Genji* into her own successful manga.

Men, too, eventually realized the potential of girl manga. Tezuka Osamu, author of the boy manga *Black Jack*, created the first long-form, or novel-length, manga for girls. *Shojo Club*, which Tezuka began in 1953, followed the adventures of Sapphire, a princess who must pretend to be a boy in order to inherit and defend her throne. Works such as these helped open the world of manga to girls and women, as both creators and audience. As a whole, girls and women remade manga to fit their sensibilities.

Japanese literature, including manga, provides accounts of social values and social changes over the last century. They reflect, too, the depth of Japanese tradition. Japanese authors tell stories about human struggles and joys, which are not limited to any one country or culture. Their literary works have entertained, educated, and captivated readers around the world.

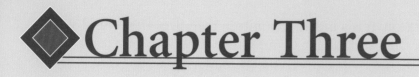

Chapter Three

The Art of Japanese Architecture

Tea plays an important role in Japan's culture. The Japanese people have used the drink for centuries as a part of their diet and as medicine. They even integrated the making of tea into the Buddhist religious tradition. Japanese architecture, too, has been influenced by tea. The story of Japanese architecture over the centuries tells how the Way of Tea became the way of the world.

The tea room inspired what came to be known as the Japanese aesthetic. For a long time, Japanese builders copied the Chinese architectural style. In the sixteenth century, however, a new, uniquely Japanese artistic sensibility began to develop—one that used natural materials and simple designs with clean lines and geometric shapes. This aesthetic became known as *wabi*. Whether in an ancient, tiny hut in the mountains or in a ground-floor garden oasis in modern Tokyo, wabi has prevailed.

In the mid-twentieth century, every Japanese city began to look the same: a crowd of tall, stark skyscrapers. A postwar population explosion and the need to quickly rebuild caused a surge in modern construction in Japan. The new construction crowded out traditional buildings, many of which were demolished. In the pursuit of urbanization, people sacrificed tradition for time.

Many Japanese architects, however, began to imprint their own heritage on modern designs. The Japanese aesthetic inspired them to create a type of architecture based on old and new, as well as native and foreign, influences. Many prominent postwar Japanese architects changed the world with their designs.

Humanizing the Modern Landscape

The need to rebuild spurred architectural innovation. Some architects focused on form, or how designs looked. Others focused on function, or how designs worked. Tange Kenzo (1913–2005) tried to blend form and function. The best example of this is his plan for the expansion of Tokyo.

Tange's "Plan for Tokyo 1960" was an attempt to solve the problems of urban crowding. After studying the patterns of people traveling to and from work, Tange created a city design that would permit growth and change. The Tokyo he envisioned would extend out over Tokyo Bay through the use of bridges, human-made islands, and floating parking. "The various architectural works will form the leaves, and the transportation and communications facilities the trunk of a great tree," Tange wrote.[23] Although the plan was never implemented, the design was considered groundbreaking.

In addition to blending form and function, Tange sought to make modern structures more welcoming. He incorporated gardens and sculptures into his designs because, as he explained, "Architecture must have something that appeals to the human heart. ... Creative work is expressed in our time as a union of technology and humanity. The role of tradition is that of a catalyst, which furthers a chemical reaction ..."[24]

Tange's use of tradition as a catalyst can be seen most clearly in two aspects of his work. His use of textures to soften the effects of concrete and steel reflect *tatami*, the straw mats found in traditional tea houses. Tange used a cantilever pillar-and-beam system that incorporated wooden timbers as a key feature in his buildings. This system had been used in ancient imperial palaces. As the Pritzker Jury noted when it awarded Tange the Pritzker Architecture Prize in 1987, "Tange arrives at shapes that lift our hearts because they seem to emerge from some ancient and dimly remembered past and yet are breathtakingly of today."[25]

Tange's works include the Hiroshima Peace Park and Center and the Olympic stadiums in Tokyo. He spent seven years (1949–1956) working on the Hiroshima Peace Park and Center. The centerpiece of the park is the Cenotaph, a giant, saddle-shaped arch under which Tange placed a chest that contains the names of those who died in the atomic bombing. His design, according to the Pritzker Jury, "made the city symbolic of the human longing for peace."[26]

Built for the 1964 Olympics, Tange's two stadiums have been called "among the most beautiful structures built in the twentieth century."[27] The semicircular structures appear delicate and almost in motion, as if they are rising up out of the ground. Still, they are strong enough to withstand the hurricanes that occur in Japan. This is another example of Tange's blending of form and function. In addition, according to one critic, these stadiums "captured the spirit of a rapidly developing Japan."[28]

Metabolism and Symbiosis

In the 1970s, a group of Japanese architects built on the ideas of Tange Kenzo to create a type of architecture called Metabolism. Metabolist architects designed buildings that could change parts according to different uses. The concept was to make buildings interchangeable and recyclable.

Kurokawa Kisho (1934–), founder of Metabolism, saw recyclable buildings as a way to reduce the environmental damage caused by modern cities. In the words of one biographer, "The limits to the development of the industrial nations are foreseeable. …[I]t was to change this exploitive lifestyle that [Kurokawa] became an architect."[29] Such concern for the environment reflects the integration of the Japanese respect for nature with modern architecture.

Kurokawa has received acclaim for his work in both the East and West. His designs include the Nagakin Capsule Tower in Tokyo, a 13-story building with 140 one-room apartments. Each apartment is attached to the building with bolts. This makes them removable and replaceable, an example of the interchangeability of Metabolist architecture. Other works include the Hiroshima City Museum of Contemporary Art, the Osaka International Convention Center, and the Illinois Sporting Club in Chicago, Illinois.

In the 1980s, Kurokawa developed the theory of Symbiosis, which he explained as a reflection of a "mix-and-match" modern world.[30] Symbiotic architecture combines elements of different cultures, as well as blending technology and nature. Kurokawa's design for the Kuala Lumpur airport in Malaysia, completed in 1998, is a prime example of Symbiosis. A high-tech, curved roof crowns the modern building, which resembles a traditional Islamic mosque. The interior features a jungle that grows in, around, and through the airport. Nature, technology, and local culture all work symbiotically in the same building.

Ecological Architecture

Ban Shigeru (1957–) is another architect whose work, in the Japanese tradition of respecting nature, expresses concern for the environment. He is renowned for his use of paper, including recycled cardboard tubes. *Time* magazine called Ban an innovator, whose "ingenious use of cardboard has redefined permanent and temporary shelter."[31]

Ban was the first architect in Japan to design a building made of mostly paper. However, he is not the first Japanese to use paper as a building tool. For centuries, the Japanese had used paper to make doors and screens called *shoji*. Ban prefers to use paper because it is inexpensive and can be easily replaced and recycled. His paper buildings are used as low-cost refugee shelters all over the world. These shelters look like log cabins because, Ban says, "[R]efugee shelter has to be beautiful. Psychologically, refugees are damaged. They have to stay in nice places."[32] The concern for others reflected in Ban's work is another aspect

Concrete Temples and Paper Doors

Japanese architecture is an art form of opposites. This is evident from comparing two types of entrances: shoji, or movable paper doors and dividers, and the Kaminari-mon, the concrete entrance to the Senso-Ji Temple in Tokyo. Though different in many ways, shoji and the entrance to Senso-Ji are both key fixtures in the Japanese architectural tradition.

Shoji doors and dividers are light and flexible. Found in homes throughout the world, shoji is signature Japanese decor. Unlike swinging doors, shoji doors slide open or fold in half to save space. These doors consist of *washi* paper over a wooden frame. Tougher than paper made from wood fibers, washi makes doors and dividers both durable and delicate.

In contrast, the Kaminari-mon, or Gate of Thunder, provides a grand entrance to an imposing building that impresses visitors with its solidity. The current temple, made from reinforced concrete, replaced one built in 1651 that was destroyed in World War II. As visitors pass through the gate, they see images of the gods of wind and thunder. Then they pass by cauldrons of incense, a towering pagoda, and statues of gold.

The Kaminari-mon gate attracts many visitors during holidays and special events, such as the Annual Asakusa Samba Carnival.

of Japanese culture, which emphasizes cooperation and collective harmony.

Preservation: A New Tradition

After World War II, the Japanese people quickly remade their nation into a modern urban landscape. By the middle of the twentieth century, Japan was home to some of the world's most modern architectural wonders. Postwar reconstruction adopted Western trends and transformed Japan's entire architectural character. Rapid construction, using concrete and steel, was an efficient way to rebuild war-torn cities and to counter urban ruin. Reconstruction and modernization came at a high cost, however. Old buildings and neighborhoods were demolished to make way for the new.

In response, Japan became a forerunner in the field of architectural preservation. Many citizens believed pre-war structures should be saved, so they organized preservation movements. Their efforts built on a tradition that dated back to the late nineteenth century, when the Japanese government had enacted the first law for the protection of cultural properties, such as artwork and buildings. Leaders passed a similar law in 1919 to protect historic places, places of scenic beauty, and national monuments. In 1950, the government combined preservation laws into one law that designated intangible cultural properties and folklore properties.

Modern preservation efforts in Japan began at the local level in the 1960s. Citizens' groups objected to the destruction of natural areas and the demolition of historic structures to make way for rapid urbanization. In turn, city governments formed their own preservation districts. The grassroots movement was successful in getting local and national preservation laws passed. Preservation districts still form a strong national network called *den-ken*. A residents' society or association has always played a key role in each district.

A Walking Tour of Japanese Folk Houses

Folk houses, or *minka*, are rustic, traditional homes that have mud-plastered or stone floors instead of raised wooden floors. In 1951, Japanese officials announced that minka would join temples, shrines, castles, and elite residences on the list of protected buildings. This was part of a new national goal, "the democratization of cultural properties."[33]

The functionality and simplicity of folk houses represents the essence of the Japanese aesthetic in architecture. This is why the city of Kawasaki started a program in 1965 to relocate folk houses all over Japan to a section called Minka-En. All twenty-five of the historic buildings at Minka-En have traditional fixtures, such as tools and utensils, to give people a sense of the past.

Visitors can get a rich sense of history from touring the homes at Minka-En. The structures include an inn for horse traders (Suzuki House), an incense shop (Ioka House), and a pharmacy (Misawa House). In addition, visitors can see the Saji Gate, which symbolized the power of an eighteenth-century samurai.

A Train Tour of the Past

The Museum Meiji-Mura, located outside Inayuma in central Japan, is an open-air museum that contains a collection of 100-year-old buildings that were once slated for demolition. Visitors may travel from one building to the next by boarding a historic locomotive or trolley cars. The museum was founded by Taniguchi Yoshiro and Tsuchikawa Moto-o. They feared that Tokyo's rush to modernization had imperiled traditional structures.

A particular point of interest is the lobby of Frank Lloyd Wright's Imperial Hotel. The hotel opened in Tokyo in 1923 and was torn down in 1968. Fortunately, preservationists rescued a portion for the museum. According to journalist Mike Meyers, "Visitors can enter the turf stone and brick remains, restored to include a coffee shop, replete with original Wright-designed furnishings. Guests often queue [line] up to slip into rented period costumes for photographs beside the fountain out front."[34]

The museum is like a movie set. Its sixty-seven buildings include post offices, police stations, butcher shops, and banks. The train starts from the Imperial Hotel lobby, goes over an iron-lattice bridge, through the gate of Kanazawa Prison, and

The Wabi of Frank Lloyd Wright

Frank Lloyd Wright was born in Wisconsin in 1867. Students and fans of Wright's work are struck by the integration of Japanese aesthetics, architecture, and philosophy in his designs. When art critics of Wright's day wrote that he derived his style from Japanese architecture, however, Wright denied a direct influence. He claimed instead that Japanese artistic principles validated his original ideas. Despite the enduring controversy, scholars see a correspondence between wabi and Wright's work. Historians cite the open spaces, horizontal lines, and the colors used by Wright as examples.

During four trips to Japan, Wright deepened his appreciation for woodblock prints and the artistry of the tea room, which he said influenced his work. Furthermore, Wright designed the Imperial Hotel in Tokyo, which opened in 1923 and was demolished in 1968. Some scholars consider the hotel evidence of the merging of two architectural traditions. "Commissioned in 1916, the hotel was to represent the emergence of Japan as a modern nation and symbolized Japan's relation to the West. To that end, Wright designed the building as a hybrid of Japanese and Western architecture."[1]

[1]Kimberly Jill Elman, Steve Knopper, and David Rifkind, "The Life and Work of Frank Lloyd Wright: Imperial Hotel, 1912–1923," *PBS Online*, http://www.pbs.org/flw/buildings/imperial/imperial.html (accessed June 16, 2007).

stops at the cathedral of St. Francis Xavier, where couples may marry. Displays inside buildings include dioramas and interactive exhibits. A kabuki troupe performs in the museum's theater.

A Global Effort

It was once common in Japan to tear down and rebuild treasured structures. After a dedicated group of citizens formed a movement to save historic buildings, preservation emerged as a new architectural tradition. This tradition became a global one, in which Japan participated as well.

In 1993, Japan nominated its first properties to be listed in the World Heritage Program, a United Nations effort to protect places of cultural and natural heritage around the world. Properties designated as heritage sites in Japan have included Buddhist monuments in the Horyu-ji area, Himeji Castle, the Shirakami Mountains, the forest at Yakushima, Itsukushima Shrine, and the Hiroshima Peace Memorial. As in all of the arts, the Japanese have worked to set their own standards against the backdrop of global preservation efforts.

A Modern "Floating World"

Kansai International Airport (KIA) was built on a human-made island in Osaka Bay, about 31 miles (50km) south of Osaka. The airport opened in 1994 and remains a marvel of modern Japanese architecture. Made of glass, steel, and concrete, KIA appears light, simple, gentle, and natural. It seems to float, reflecting the Japanese "floating world" artistic ideal of the nineteenth century. This effect is no accident. Architects wanted to remain true to Japanese tradition while using modern technology and materials to move travelers as safely and efficiently as possible.

Destination: KIA

KIA is what an international airport should be, according to architect Renzo Piano, who designed the facility. He thought modern airports were confusing and dehumanizing, so he created a structure that would be pleasant and easy to navigate.

Visitors to KIA encounter a unique airport experience. There is no maze of boxes, as in many international airports. Travelers do not have to read signs to find their way. Piano designed KIA to be a place where "people can walk to the destination while intuitively knowing their positions."[35]

The roof seems to ripple in the wind, due to its wavelike contour. Inside, the roof's high curves match the path that cooled air takes from one end of the facility to the other, rising in a long arc and then falling in a shorter one. Piano designed the roof as a *fractal*, or a geometric shape made of smaller copies of itself.

The roof's geometry mimicked fractals found in the airport's natural surroundings, such as clouds, mountains, and

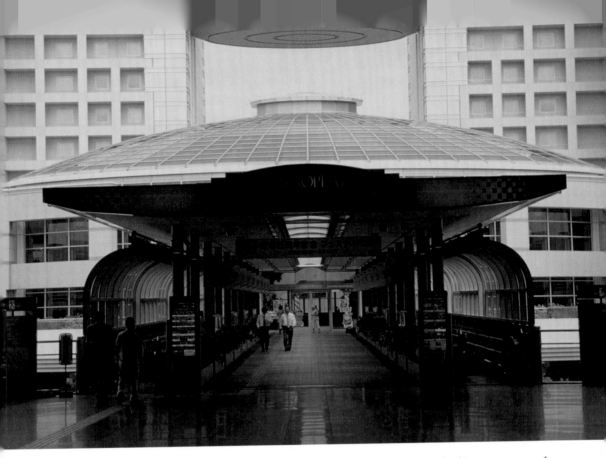

Technology is a key feature of Kansai International Airport, including automated walkways at the international terminal.

waves. Piano's plan placed the fractal shape of the airport onto the fractal-rich natural landscape. His goal was to illustrate how architectural design could combine urban life and nature.

In keeping with that goal, "the airport's architectural expression incorporates many natural elements," according to one visitor.[36] These elements include trees, wind, and light. Trees line the airport's huge entryway, which is called the canyon. Wind is the prevailing theme in the spacious check-in area. Artificial wind, a wind channel, a mobile sculpture,

and an iron railing make visitors feel like they are being carried along to the boarding gates. The large, open boarding area is flooded with light, and planes outside are visible at all hours.

Piano wanted to engage travelers' senses and enrich their souls. He achieved his goal by making the airport a sensory experience from start to finish. Journalist Suzuki Hiroyuki marveled that the first time he visited the airport, he heard classical piano music playing. He writes, "The sound of the piano will continue to flow with the trees, wind, light, people and information which move through the building. I wonder if the story of the new airport is just too perfect."[37]

A Meta-Airport

The KIA transportation system was designed to provide stepping stones to various destinations in Japan. A network of boat, ferry, bus, and train lines connects the island airport to cities across the water. As Japan's second-largest airport, Kansai was intended to boost the Osaka region's economy by connecting it with international economies as well.

KIA made this region of Japan an increasingly important center for international business. The world's economic community began to conduct more business at meta-airports such as Kansai, which offered more than airline service. These airports often included meeting rooms, exhibition and showroom facilities, business centers, and other spaces.

Flights of Fancy

Just as Kansai International Airport engages the senses, its creative design inspires the imagination. From the sky, the structure looks like a seaport. Piano wanted the airport to be as welcome a sight to air passengers as port cities were to ancient sailors. He compared travelers to KIA to "fishermen seeing an island for the first time after a long voyage."[1] The wavy roof matches the airport's surroundings. According to Suzuki Hiroyuki, "The gently undulating center of the building can be aptly compared to small islands floating on a vast island."[2]

In contrast to many other airports, KIA looks futuristic and surreal. From the sky, glowing in the middle of a darkened sea at night, the airport looks like some kind of spaceship.

On the ground, the airport's structure has proven just as intriguing. "When you land at the airport, the building from outside looks like a sleeping kite, a gentle object," Piano once said.[3] In the design phase, many people compared the slats of the airport's framework to the bones of a giant dinosaur. The airport has been said to resemble a bird, an insect, and a butterfly.

[1]Suzuki Hiroyuki, "Trees, Wind, Light, and Sound," *Process Architecture, Kansai International Airport Passenger Terminal Building* (Tokyo: Process Architecture Ltd., 1994), 15.
[2]Ibid.
[3]"Of Monuments, Machines and Temporality," *Process Architecture, Kansai International Airport Passenger Terminal Building* (Tokyo: Process Architecture Ltd., 1994), 10.

The location of Kansai served another practical purpose. The mountainous, densely populated mainland had no room for a new international airport.

Pride of Japan and the World

Piano believed that airports such as Kansai International should be as impressive as the grand cathedrals and train stations of the past. "They [train stations] were meeting places, a reference point, a place where people congregated, and a place of adventure," Piano said in an interview.[38] He designed KIA to resemble a train station, which was usually made of two parts. One part was a large building open to the public, and the other part, in the back, was a shedlike structure that housed the trains. Similarly, KIA's large, open reception area receives visitors and travelers, while in the back, jets and planes stay ready for flight. Furthermore, Piano believed that train stations were "an expression of the sense of pride of the city."[39] He felt that airports such as KIA should be admired at home and abroad as architectural achievements. In regard to that idea, "Kansai International represents Osaka well to the world," writes one observer.[40]

To Piano, airports needed to exceed the place train stations held in society in one crucial sense: they had to be open to the world, as part of a network of airports, belonging "to the place but at the same time it belongs to the earth."[41] In addition, "Airports connect one country to another, and are the places where people take their first steps in a foreign country."[42] Therefore, Piano felt that airports must be sites of international cultural exchange. In this way, KIA is a microcosm of Japanese culture, which has participated in cultural exchanges for centuries.

Kansai International has been resilient through typhoons and earthquakes. Still, the airport is sinking faster than expected, and engineers are working on a plan to raise the seawall.

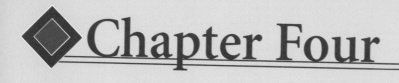

Chapter Four

The Performing Arts in Japan

Japanese artists who participate in the performing arts are not mimicking Western performances. They are directly involved in international artistic movements, which are in return greatly affected by their participation. Performance arts, such as jazz and theater, have entertained audiences in Japan since the 1920s. Modern forms of performance art, such as hip-hop music, co-exist with more traditional Japanese forms, such as Kabuki. Japanese performers have adapted international art forms, including hip-hop and jazz, and infused them with uniquely Japanese elements.

Kabuki

Created as the first form of Japanese entertainment for the common people, Kabuki was the dominant dramatic art in Japan for four centuries. Kabuki performances incorporated dance, music, acrobatics, mimicry, and spectacular staging and costumes. The word *Kabuki* may come from the verb *kabuku*, which means "to lean" or "to be out of the ordinary," so Kabuki could mean experimental or bizarre theater. The expression *Kabuki-mono* referred to wild gangs of young urban eccentrics who wore outrageous clothes and had strange hairstyles.

A woman invented Kabuki in the early seventeenth century. Okuni, a female dancer, assembled a group of traveling female dancers and actors. Ironically, women were barred from Kabuki almost as soon as Okuni began it.

The seductive style of the Kabuki dances bothered government officials. They viewed Kabuki as a corruption of women's virtue and banned women from performing. Young boys dressed as women then performed the programs. This type of Kabuki was banned because of moral concerns as well. Older men as-

The Tokyo Ballet has performed in more than 30 countries around the world, and given more overseas performances than any other performing arts group in Japanese history.

sumed Kabuki roles from then on, but the association between Kabuki and immorality persisted.

In Kabuki, a storyteller narrated the major action. Performers delivered lines of dialogue, chanted, and played the *samisen*, a three-stringed instrument similar to a guitar. Actors used artificially high-pitched voices, made exaggerated gestures, and wore elaborate costumes and makeup. Trapdoors, revolving stages, and runways added to the excitement. Kabuki was highly interactive. Actors addressed the audience. The audience members shouted their praise and clapped their hands according to a certain pattern.

Kabuki themes came from history, legend, and community life. For example, the work of Chikamatsu Monzaemon (1653–1725), known as the Shakespeare of Japan, focused on the conflict between personal

Villagers in Hinoemata, in central Japan, have been performing Kabuki for more than 200 years.

desires and the Confucian concept of loyalty and duty. Another common theme was *kanzen-choaku*, which means "reward the virtuous and punish the wicked." A full Kabuki performance consisted of a historical play, a domestic play, intervening dance plays, and a dance finale. Plays included ghosts, courtesans, and other unusual characters.

Modern masters updated Kabuki, and some actors attracted large audiences. Ichikawa Ennosuke III (1939–), for example, became famous for his acting skills, clever acrobatics, fast costume changes, and magical illusions. Two major Kabuki theaters today are the Kabuki-Za Theater and the National Theatre, both in Tokyo. The Kabuki-Za Theater emphasizes the actor's role in Kabuki plays, while the National Theatre emphasizes the plays themselves.

Takarazuka Turnabout

Established in 1913, the all-female Takarazuka Revue Company was the counterpart to male Kabuki. Hundreds of women joined this theatrical company. Women made up about 90 percent of its fan base.

In Takarazuka productions, women play male characters. These women are called *otokoyaku*. Some critics objected to the use of otokoyaku. Western audiences sometimes found "something not quite right" about Takarazuka's use of otokoyaku.[43] Nonetheless, Takarazuka won worldwide respect as a way for girls and women to express themselves in a male-dominated society. As one reviewer said, "the *otokoyaku* represent a vicarious way for young women to live out fantasies of strength and power. But what they really come for is romance, the pure, old-fashioned, fairy-tale variety. So Takarazuka gives them just that, clear-cut stories full of romance and spectacle but devoid of crudity or passion, much as Disney sugar-coats its love stories."[44]

Still popular today, Takarazuka features elaborate musical productions, love stories, and foreign settings. Takarazuka's repertoire shows that this Japanese art form has become an international one. Productions include Japanese-style classical dramas and histories, such as *The Tale of Genji*; European-style and Broadway-based performances, such as *West Side Story*; and folk dances from all over the world.

The Takarazuka Music School, which trains teenage girls in acting, singing, dancing, music, and theater history, only accepts between forty and fifty students a year. Competition is fierce among applicants. The school's daily routine is rigorous. Besides attending classes, students are expected to clean dorms and classrooms and meet inspections.

Noh Talent

Noh is Kabuki's older sibling and is, in fact, the oldest existing form of Japanese theater. The Noh style evolved from a combination of Chinese performance art and Japanese dance. It was originally an art form exclusively for Japan's samurai class. Laws prevented commoners from learning the music and dance of Noh. As the era of samurai privilege ended, Noh became popular among the general public.

Noh was unique because it emphasized storytelling rather than re-enacting. Compared to Kabuki, Noh was sedate—very little happened in a Noh play. Performers used their appearance, dancelike movements, and a sparsely decorated background to tell a story that the audience already knew. Artist Paul Binnie explains:

In 2006, the Takarazuka Revue performed The Rose of Versailles, *about the eighteenth-century French queen Marie-Antoinette.*

In general, Japanese Noh plays are not very dramatic, although they are beautiful, since the text is full of poetical allusions and the dances, though slow, are extremely elegant. It is this very beauty that makes Noh a living art form still, over six hundred years after it developed, and which has caused all subsequent Japanese theatrical forms to draw on aspects of Noh.[45]

Noh actors wore standardized masks to indicate which traditional roles they were playing. Every Noh play had three major roles: the principal actor, the subordinate actor, and the narrator. Musicians and a chorus backed these three performers. Sometimes lesser roles were included as well. Each role was considered a specialty and had its own place on the Noh stage. In fact, the word *noh* means "ability" or "skill." All Noh participants received special training to acquire the skills they needed to correctly perform the dramas.

One of the most important elements of any Noh performance was the reading of the story. The scripts for most plays identify which character speaks each line. Noh scripts identified how the words should be spoken and what gestures or dance movements should accompany them.

Most Noh stories involved legends or tragic histories. The stories can be divided into five types: the *kami* (god) play, the fighting play, the wig play, the mad-woman play, the final, or demon, play, and the present-day play. This last type tended to be more realistic than the other types, which often included mythical or supernatural elements. All Noh stories were short, so most performances consisted of three plays, each of a different type. Comic acts between the plays helped lighten the mood. Every Noh performance began with a dance-prayer for peace and prosperity.

Along with masks, actors wear elaborate costumes to help capture the audience's imagination during the slow, solemn movements of a Noh performance.

Noh Sweat!

In the United States, Indiana University of Pennsylvania offers training in the Noh dramatic arts through the Noh Training Project. For six hours a day, three weeks each summer, students undergo rigorous training in *utai* (the chant), *shimai* (the dance), and *hayashi* (musical instruments) of Noh. They watch performances and learn about the literary, musical, and historical aspects of Noh. A recital ends the workshop.

Student Charlie Hensley describes the Noh workshop as "enervating, exhilarating, soul-challenging, callus-inducing, life-changing . ... Noh kidding."[1] One shimai position, called *seiza*, requires performers to sit on their heels. This proved particularly grueling for Hensley. "The pain is excruciating after a few minutes, since our ankles carry most of our weight directly to the floor. ... With practice, I'm grateful to find my legs fall asleep, so there's really no pain—until I try to stand. Over time, calluses build up on my ankles and I can spend more time each day in *seiza*."[2]

Hensley says that training in Noh gave him a new view of theater and a "powerful joy." He writes, "I was a baby learning to crawl. It felt good."[3]

[1]Charlie Hensley, "No business Like Noh Business," *American Theatre*, January 1, 2000, http://216.239.51.104/search?q=cache:hmIus7S39C4J:www.mona.uwi.edu/liteng/courses/e10f/documents/noh%2520theatre%2520for%2520beginners.doc+kamae+in+Japanese+theater&hl=en&ct=clnk&cd=2&gl=us&client=safari (accessed July 15, 2007).
[2]Ibid.
[3]Ibid.

About two thousand Noh plays have survived into the modern era. Zeami, a playwright considered to be the founder of Noh, wrote most of the plays sometime during the Ashikaga Period (1336–1600). Two main factors contributed to the plays' survival. The first was the preservation of Noh texts, which contain the words, music, and movements necessary for a performance. The second was the direct training in Noh performing skills.

Noh has experienced some changes in recent years. New passages have been added to some plays to spotlight lesser roles. Playwrights such as Mishima Yukio (1925–1970) have written new dramas that follow the themes of the old plays. In the 1980s, Noh was exported to the Vatican, where a Christian Noh drama written by a university professor was performed for the pope. As Binnie concluded, "[Noh] is a truly timeless art form, which speaks to modern audiences as it did to the noblemen and women of the [Ashikaga] period."[46]

Geisha, Then and Now

Geisha were professionally trained female artists who lived and worked in special districts called *karyukai*. Meaning "the flower and the willow world," such places were reserved for the "enjoyment of aesthetic pleasure," according to former geisha Iwasaki Mineko.[47] In fact, the word *geisha* means "artist." In many ways, geisha themselves were living works of art.

The traditional art of geisha was infused with *iki*, which may be defined as "spirit" or "life," and how fashion or art expresses one's lifestyle. Iki came to reflect the style of "someone possessing wealth but not attached to it, familiar with sensual pleasures but not a slave to them, and aware of current fads but able to rise above them."[48]

Geisha were entertainers who recited verse, played musical instruments, and engaged in light conversation. Today, geisha perform traditional Japanese music, song, and dance in places such as the Gion Kobu Kaburen-jo theatre in Kyoto. Iwasaki summarizes the job of the geisha in this way: "We are highly trained professional artists whose mission is to preserve the best in traditional Japanese culture."[49]

Girls had to complete three stages of strict training to become geisha. In the first stage, called *shikomi*, young girls arrived at the geisha house, or *okiya*. They worked as maids, waited on senior geisha, and received lessons in traditional dialect and dress. To enter the second stage, called *minarai*, the girls had to pass an exam. If they passed, they no longer had to do housework. They learned teahouse practices, attended parties, and practiced geisha social techniques, such as conversation and games. This stage lasted about a month. In the final stage, trainees became *maiko*, or apprentice geisha. A maiko learned from a mentor called *onee-san* (older sister) and accompanied her to engagements. In this relationship, the onee-san taught the maiko everything about the geisha arts, including serving tea, playing the samisen, and making conversation. After an apprenticeship that could be as short as six months or as long as five years, the maiko was promoted to a full-fledged geisha.

Today, geisha are relatively rare. Iwasaki believes this traditional art form must be more open if it is to continue: "I think it is crucial that the tradition survive as a living testament to the greatness of classical Japanese culture. It has to become easier for the general population to have access to the world of the geisha if it is to survive. I think there should be more events, organized by the Performers Association, where anyone who wants to can experience geisha culture up close."[50]

Jazu

African American artists created jazz music, which quickly spread to Europe and Asia. By the 1920s, jazz dominated the club scene not only in urban Japan, but in the Japanese colonial cities of Shanghai, China, and Seoul, Korea. To some people, however, jazz did not seem

Sit-Down Comedy

Rakugo is the 300-year-old traditional art of Japanese storytelling. University professor and rakugo comedian Kimie Oshima calls it sit-down comedy, in contrast to stand-up comedy. Both forms of comedy have the same goal: to make people laugh. In rakugo, a comic sits on a cushion to tell funny stories and make funny faces. Rakugo is now a popular Japanese cultural export, often performed in English.

Oshima believes that rakugo teaches the world about Japanese culture in an amusing way. Rakugo jokes and puns are often unique to Japanese culture, however, which can make translation difficult. The comedian speaks in Japanese and then immediately in English, trying to maintain the essence of the original words.

To address the stereotype that the Japanese are a humorless people, Oshima tells a joke. "We do have some sense of humor. But Japanese export too many good products like cars and stereos. So we just decided not to export good jokes."[1]

Oshima and other rakugo artists hope that anyone who attends a rakugo show will no longer believe that the Japanese do not have a sense of humor.

[1] Quoted in Kimie Oshima, "Spreading the Rakugo Word," *What's Rakugo*, http://www.english-rakugo.com/english_version/english_what.html (accessed July 15, 2007).

like a good fit with Japanese culture. Many believed that the Japanese "can't swing."[51] Despite the critics, Japanese jazz—called *jazu*—thrived as a distinct musical genre.

Japanese culture and jazz were, in reality, compatible. One music fan gave this opinion about jazz's role in Japanese society: "Mix Dynamite [a jazz group] … opened my mind to the possibility that jazz could be real in Japan, that it could be more than a superficial bauble [decoration] demonstrating urbane sophistications and faux [fake] hipness, but rather could fill holes in people's lives that empowered them to scream out in joy and anguish."[52]

French and American movies with jazz musical scores "triggered a Jazz boom" in Japan.[53] On a more personal level, jazz came to Japan through musicians, such as pianist Shigeya Kikuhi. Shigeya heard jazz when he traveled to cities in the United States. After coming upon a street performance in Chicago, he dedicated his career to learning to play jazz the way he had heard it played there. Shigeya's dedication inspired other musicians to master the jazz sound as well.

During World War II, however, Japanese leaders outlawed jazz, forcing musi-

When U.S. forces occupied Japan at the end of World War II, U.S. soldiers mingled with Japanese young people at military clubs and nightclubs where jazz music was played.

cians to play their music in secret. Jazz historian E. Taylor Atkins explains, "[T]he authorities assumed a hardened public attitude toward jazz on Japanese soil. But enforcement and compliance remained haphazard [random] and, at most, jazz musicians merely had to exercise more prudent [careful] judgment."[54] Basically, they'd play 'sizzling hot jazz' in sizzling hot quarters—homes or businesses with windows shut to muffle the sound.

During the U.S. occupation after the war, Japanese jazz musicians both embraced American trends and tried to break free from them. Not surprisingly, jazz, with its "dangerous aura," appealed to rebellious teens most of all, just as it had in the 1920s.[55]

In essence, jazz cafés were similar to the nineteenth-century entertainment districts (ukiyo) of Edo Japan. Both offered patrons an escape from an overbearing society. Both began during a time of increasing militarization. Both relied on

Chigusa's Legacy

Jazz cafés retained a uniquely Japanese character. Professor Michael Molasky describes the scene at a jazz café named Chigusa:

> Filled with sound, smoke, and hundreds of records, jazz coffeehouses used to be a space for young people who came looking for a proper understanding of the music. ... Chigusa was a place of learning and of comfort. The unspoken rules, which they followed faithfully, included listening to the music in silence and waiting in turn to make a request, jotting it down on a scrap of paper.[1]

By listening silently and taking turns to make requests, Chigusa's patrons exhibited the traditional Japanese concerns about community and respect for others, even as they enjoyed a very nontraditional form of music.

The development of portable music and a loss of interest in traditional jazz caused many jazz cafés to close, including Chigusa. Perhaps, however, the cafés will not completely disappear. In an article about Chigusa's closing, journalist Wakao Aiko quoted one of the café's last visitors as saying, "I am sure there are people out there who would love to take on a place like this, or at least, carry on the tradition. ... It has such a wonderful atmosphere."[2]

[1]Wakao Aiko, "Japan jazz fans bid sad farewell to historic café," *washingtonpost. com*, January 27, 2007, http://www.washingtonpost.com/wp-dyn/content/article/2007/01/27/AR2007012701603.html (accessed July 15, 2007).
[2]Ibid.

---

mass media for promotion—woodblock prints promoted the ukiyo, and jazz recordings promoted jazz cafés. In both cases, the art form spurred cultural change. The Mix Dynamite fan might have been describing both Edo teahouses and jazz cafés when he wrote: "Here you let all that mess hang out."[56]

Japanese young people have rediscovered jazz. Club jazz, or *nu-jazz*, showcases the talents of Japanese DJs such as Ryota Nozaki (Jazztronik), brothers Okino Shuya and Okino Yoshihiro of Kyoto Jazz Massive, and Toshio Matsuura. Nu-jazz artists such as Sleepwalker and Groove-Line have transformed traditional jazz in Japan.

In general, jazz is thriving in Japan. Like other art forms, Japanese jazz has successfully set itself apart as it has absorbed international trends.

Kabuki Hip-Hop

Kabuki hip-hop, or Japanese hip-hop, is in its third decade. According to scholar Dr. Ian Condry, a showing of the film *Wild Style* in Tokyo in 1983 inspired early Japanese hip-hop performers. The film portrays the life of a graffiti artist in New York City and features rap artists and break-dancers. Some of the film's stars traveled to Japan to promote the movie and performed in Tokyo department stores. Japanese dancers followed their lead, break-dancing in Tokyo's Yoyogi Park on Sundays with other performers.

The next step in the evolution of Japanese hip-hop, according to Dr. Condry, was that DJs had begun to perform on the radio by 1985. The first all-hip-hop club opened in Tokyo in 1986. Dr. Condry believes that rap music was slower to catch on because "many in the music world doubted that it would be possible to rap in Japanese, that is, to be able to perform with the needed flow (rhythmic nuance) and rhymes. ..."[57] Japanese rappers proved skeptics wrong when they began to invent their own flows and rhyming styles.

During the 1990s, Japanese hip-hop grew more popular. Music from the United States influenced many artists, but innovative Japanese performers contributed to the genre as well.

One major consideration for performers and fans of Japanese hip-hop was the effect this new genre had on the nation's identity and unique culture. To some, hip-hop diminished Japanese culture. Others looked at the issue in a different way. In Dr. Condry's words, "[W]hat if hip-hop is used to express one's Japaneseness?"[58] He provides as an example a song by Kohei, who sings about eating "'rice, not bread, and fish, not meat' and so on, riffing on the notion that being hip-hop and being Japanese are mutually exclusive."[59]

Japanese hip-hop has become a significant social and artistic forum, in which "poor Japanese found a voice."[60] Kabuki hip-hop focuses on global political issues, finding kinship with African American hip-hop. As Dr. Condry explained in an interview: "They say they're into black culture. They say, 'I don't care about America per se. But I love Spike Lee movies and I read the autobiography of Malcolm X ... and I appreciate what black Americans have struggled to achieve.'"[61]

Japanese hip-hop is definitely setting its own course, however. Performers sing the songs in Japanese, not in English. Songs have almost no lyrics about guns and little mention of drugs. Instead, Kabuki hip-hop lyrics often incorporate samurai lore, and the music is sometimes performed Kabuki style. Just as they did with jazz, Japanese artists have adapted a Western art form to express their own unique style.

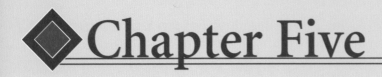

Chapter Five

Japanese Cinema

Cinema in Japan began, as it did throughout the world, with the invention of the kinetoscope in the nineteenth century. Japanese filmmakers then began to create a uniquely Japanese cinema. In fact, the first subjects of Japanese films—geishas—could have been found nowhere else but Japan. The next subjects were Japanese actors, which made film a natural extension of the nation's thriving theater arts.

Japanese filmmakers never lost sight of their heritage. As critics Joseph Anderson and Donald Richie observed, "one of the last film industries to create a national style, the Japanese is now one of the last to retain it."[62] Even though Japanese cinema was part of an international art form, it remained representative of Japanese culture. As the decades passed, Japanese filmmakers influenced world cinema as well.

During the twentieth century, Japanese cinematic artists asserted themselves in three distinct movements. In classic Japanese cinema, directors such as Kurosawa Akira earned international acclaim. About mid-century, "oddball" filmmakers often added subtle and sometimes shocking elements to their movies. By the end of the century, Japanese animators had embraced an array of new techniques. They created an entirely new art form, anime, which relied on Japanese tradition as much as the classic films had. Japanese cinema had come full circle in its first one hundred years.

Large billboards in Japan advertise Japanese movies as well as American movies that have been translated for Japanese audiences.

Classic Japanese Cinema: Star Directors Shine

Japanese filmmakers were like filmmakers around the world: their creativity and originality led to new techniques and genres. Kurosawa Akira, considered by many to be one of world's greatest film directors, believed that directors were the ones who gave a nation's cinema its unique characteristics. "In any film industry, [it is] only the work of a dedicated few that is responsible for whatever enduring value that country's film art may have. This has been as true in Japan as anywhere else," Kurosawa said.[63]

In the West, film directors usually controlled production from the very beginning. Eventually, movie companies, especially in the United States, adopted the producer system. In this system, directors and producers shared control of production. In Japan, however, the opposite was true. Directors had little authority at first. Gradually, the Japanese director's importance grew. By the middle of the twentieth century, Japanese cinema operated under the director system. Directors often wrote, edited, acted in, and produced the films they directed. According to Joseph Anderson and Donald Richie, "today the Japanese film director, as far as having the final say goes, is among the strongest in the world."[64] Japan's first film directors have earned acclaim as some of the world's finest. Many Japanese films made during the twentieth century are considered among the best in world cinema.

Mizoguchi Kenji: A Reel Realist

Mizoguchi Kenji (1898–1956), known by the nickname Goteken, began to earn a living as a performing artist early in life. He worked for the production company Nikkatsu as an actor and specialized in playing female roles. Mizoguchi directed his first film in 1922.

As a director, Mizoguchi used his experience playing female roles to create portrayals of strong female characters. He did this long before women's liberation movements arose around the world in the 1960s. Two of Mizoguchi's best-known films are *Osaka Elegy* and *Sisters of the Gion*, both from 1936. The films not only presented strong female characters, but expressed a "social philosophy implicitly opposed to what was happening in Japan at the moment,"[65] referring to Japan's pursuit of empire and movement away from tradition.

Mizoguchi expressed this philosophy through realistic portrayals of everyday life in Japan. *Osaka Elegy*, for example, "carried realism to an extreme never before seen in Japan. No longer did reality have to be twisted to prove a point. Here, reality was presented on its own terms. … The viewer could look at a situation and judge for himself."[66] Mizoguchi reportedly asked that the script for *Sisters of the Gion* "portray people so real that the audience could smell their body odor."[67] Many regarded the film as the best prewar movie made in Japan, but officials censored it for being immoral.

Mizoguchi was known for his loyalty to the values of the Mejii Period (1868–1912). His films showed the growing conflict between traditional and modern forces that began in the late nineteenth century. In *Osaka Elegy*, for example, a girl struggles with the modernization of Osaka. *Sisters of the Gion* tells the story of two sisters, one who is old-fashioned and one who is more modern.

Mizoguchi's style reflected a new realism. He showed that Japan was in danger of losing its traditions, but he did not romanticize Japan's past. As one critic noted, "while others saw the [Meiji] period through the dim eyes of extreme nostalgia, Mizoguchi's was a sharp, clear, and realistic view."[68] When Mizoguchi died, director Kurosawa Akira paid him this tribute: "Now that Mizoguchi is gone, there are very few directors left who can see the past clearly and realistically."[69]

Ozu Yasujiro: Japan's Most Japanese

Ozu Yasujiro (1903–1963) contributed to ninety-one films over five decades. Considered to be one of the twentieth century's great filmmakers, he rejected foreign cinematic trends. "I have formulated my own directing style in my head, proceeding without any unnecessary imitation of others," Ozu said of his work.[70] He is considered by many Japanese to be the most Japanese of all directors.

Ozu's major theme was family life. In fact, "his films so faithfully reflect Japanese life that—more than any other director—Ozu is the spokesman for both the older and the younger generations."[71] Ozu considered the script the most important aspect of filmmaking, and he rarely used special effects. His films have "none of the violent action and therefore none of the breakneck pace so common in motion pictures."[72]

Ozu focused on characters. His works often depicted family tensions, as in *Tokyo Story* (1953) and *Tokyo Twilight* (1957). *Tokyo Story* tells of an elderly couple's effort to visit their adult children. The children, however, are less than welcoming of their parents. The story of *Tokyo Twilight* follows two sisters whose long-lost mother returns to them.

The dialogue in Ozu's films won high acclaim. According to Anderson and Richie, "Ozu's characters always say what is appropriate to the situation, as if their conversation were stolen directly from life."[73]

Kurosawa Akira: West Meets East

If Ozu Yasujiro is Japan's most Japanese director, Kurosawa Akira (1910–1998) might be Japan's least Japanese director. In the words of Anderson and Richie,

Kurosawa has always deliberately refused to make the expected kind of picture. He has consistently… [refused] to accept the prevailing philosophy of the Japanese film. Rather, he has sought and found

The film Tokyo Story *featured actresses Kyôko Kagawa (left) and Setsuko Hara (right).*

originality. …He is "Western" in that he is perhaps the only Japanese director who can be called a creator in the pioneer sense of the word.[74]

In a career that lasted seven decades, Kurosawa worked as a writer, an editor, a director, and a producer on 157 films. His specialties were Shakespearean adaptations and samurai stories. Kurosawa's films are known for their technical brilliance and tender humanism. Commenting that a filmmaker says "only one thing," Kurosawa remarked, "If I look objectively at my pictures I have made, I think I say: 'Why can't human beings try to be happier?'"[75]

Kurosawa began working in the film industry in 1936 as an assistant director. He directed his first movie in 1943. The turning point in Kurosawa's career was *Rashomon* (1950). In the story, set in twelfth-century Japan, a bandit is acc-

LION D'ARGENT - MEILLEUR REALISATEUR
FESTIVAL VENISE 2003

ZAToich

un
Takes

sparked a wave of American adaptations of Japanese horror movies, including the films of Shimizu Takashi.

In 2004, *The Grudge*, a remake of the Japanese hit *Ju-On*, was released in the United States. Both films are about how a curse afflicts characters who die while in a terrible rage. The curse does not end with their deaths, nor do their vengeful feelings. According to critic Stefan Lovgren, the success of *The Grudge* "moved the Japanese horror (J-horror) movie genre to the front of the Hollywood cue [sic]."[78]

Despite the crossover success of *The Grudge*, there are key differences between the U.S. horror genre and J-horror. The stories in J-horror movies are surreal, not realistic. They are irrational, not rational. According to Lovgren, these movies possess "a subtlety and restraint foreign to most U.S. horror."[79] Japanese horror films move slowly compared to the fast-paced, action-packed U.S. horror genre. "Japanese directors are considered masters at using silence and empty spaces to create an impending sense of doom and dread," Lovgren explains.[80]

Traditional folklore, ghost stories, and myths had always inspired Japanese cinema to some degree. After World War II, however, Japanese films began to reflect modern worries. In essence, horror movies came to express a national psychology of increasing anxiety. Lovgren cites Stuart Galbraith IV, a film historian who lives in Kyoto, to explain how films came to portray the unease many Japanese felt. "In Japan this unease is impolite to express in public, Galbraith said, but the anxiety is reflected in Japan-

Special Effects

The field of special effects is both controversial and prized within the world film industry. Computer-generated or computer graphics imagery (CGI) is an important component of anime, television production, and video game technology.

Supporters of CGI, and of special effects in general, credit this technology with expanding the art of film to include elements never before possible. They believe that CGI technology opens the field of special effects to those who would otherwise be shut out due to economics.

Opponents of CGI have challenged the growing reliance on this technology. Shimizu Takashi, director of *Ju-On* and *The Grudge*, has stated: "As soon as they [the audience] figure out that it's a CGI, it's not going to be scary. . . . If people are not going to be scared of those CGI, I'd rather just do it practically . . . ."[1]

[1]Stacy Layne, "The Grudge 2: Interview with Takashi Shimizu," *horror.com*, http://www.horror.com/php/article-1201-1.html (accessed June 2, 2007).

Shimizu Takashi's film, Ju-On, *was shown in almost 30 countries.*

ese horror movies."[81] As people's anxieties increased, so did the graphic nature of Japanese cinema.

Despite the popularity of oddball, J-horror, and new cinema works in the West, critics and filmmakers agreed that Western remakes could never completely replicate the Japanese originals. The unique nature of Japan's cinema appeared to have endured yet another era of outside influences.

Anime: Japanese Artists Refine a New Fine Art

Anime, or Japanese animation, is more than just cartoons. It has become an art form unto itself, one that incorporates elements of both ancient and modern Japanese culture. Anime sometimes addresses controversial social issues, and it appeals to people of all ages. In fact, anime makes up about half of all Japanese films. This is a significant difference from the West, where most films are live action. In recent years, anime has become popular around the world, providing a unique window into Japanese culture for an international audience.

Although many people are just discovering anime, it is not a new form of animation. From the first anime export in 1917, Seitaro Kitayama's *Momotaro*, Japanese anime artists have worked to see that their art form is recognized alongside other major artistic traditions. "Not only has Japanese animation been part of the world all along, but the world has always been part of Japanese animation," Michael Arnold writes.[82] Despite anime's use of "ethnically-neutral" characters, the genre has featured stories and characters "drenched in stereotypically Japanese images" for decades.[83] All in all, anime's appeal may be due to its "hybridity," to use Arnold's term.[84]

As an art form, anime has inspired serious academic review, just like the more established arts. While some critics dwell on anime's violent elements, others find

The Mach 5 car from the anime film Speed Racer *(2008).*

a rich store of historical and literary subjects. Many anime films and television shows, for example, are based on manga. As was the case with manga, author Susan Napier sees anime as an expression of how people feel about a rapidly changing world: "Indeed, anime may be the perfect medium to capture what is perhaps the overriding issue of our day, the shifting nature of identity in a constantly changing society. With its rapid shifts of narrative pace and its constantly transforming imagery, the animated medium is superbly positioned to illustrate the atmosphere of change."[85]

Napier makes an excellent case for anime's universal appeal. Even in the United States, home of some of the world's most recognizable animated characters, anime such as *Pokémon, Sailor Moon, Gundam Wing,* and *Yugi-Oh* seems to have exceeded Mickey Mouse and Bugs Bunny in popularity. Napier explains this by quoting a female psychology student who said, "'Disney animation is pretty,' but it lacks the emotion of 'anime.'"[86]

Anime is a unique reflection of Japanese

culture and enriches the lives of audiences everywhere. Although it is a comparatively young art form, like its young characters, it has increasingly drawn the attention of critics and scholars and displayed a depth and significance unusual for such a new phenomenon.

Miyazaki Hayao: Anime's Champion

One of Japan's greatest animation directors is Miyazaki Hayao (1941–). Called the Japanese Walt Disney, he is one of anime's most productive and beloved figures. His film *Mononoke-hime* (*Princess Mononoke*, 1997) received the Japanese equivalent of the Academy Award for Best Film. Extremely popular in Japan, his works have received international acclaim as well. His appeal extends beyond his films' commercial success. His talent and humanity as an artist are recognized at home and abroad.

A number of characteristics make Miyazaki's animation appeal to children and adults alike. His films often involve characters who fly. Children play key roles. Stories have mysterious settings, such as the floating islands of *Castle in the Sky* (1986), the forests in *Princess Mononoke*, and the spirit land in *Spirited Away* (2001). At the same time, Miyazaki's films address serious adult issues, such as nature, ecology, and pollution.

A champion of working people, Miyazaki portrays Japanese traditions in a new way. "When I talk about traditions, I'm not talking about temples, which we got from China anyway. There is an indigenous Japan, and elements of that are what I'm trying to capture in my work," he says.[87] Although a pessimist by nature, Miyazaki makes films with positive messages. He wants his stories to provide more than mere entertainment. As a serious animator and proud Japanese citizen, he aspires to connect the past to the present, to make a better future for children and adults in Japan and around the

In 2006, animation director Miyazaki Hayao was named one of the most influential Asians of the past 60 years by Time *magazine.*

Samurai Champloo

Samurai Champloo (2004), a Japanese anime television series directed by Watanabe Shinichiro (1965–), is the "hippest, baddest anime title of them all," according to Theron Martin of the Anime News Network.[1] The series is aptly named, signifying a mix of styles, cultures, and historical periods. *Champloo* comes from the Okinawan word *chanpur*, which means "to mix or blend." The series tells the story of Mugen, a warrior and break-dancer, and Jin, a traditional fighter. The two samurai put aside their differences after a teahouse waitress, Fuu, rescues them from execution. She invites them to join her on a quest to find a samurai who smells like sunflowers. The setting for the action-packed story is the Meiji period, when modernization led to the end of the samurai warrior class.

Fans and critics praise the music and hip attitude of *Samurai Champloo*. The music is a combination of hip-hop and rhythm and blues, enhanced by music-video-style editing in the animation. Content is violent and suggestive, but not explicit. "This isn't one for the kiddies, but teenagers would probably love it. It's easy to see why it has already made such an impression on the American fan community," Martin writes.[2]

[1]Theron Martin, review of *Samurai Champloo*, DVD 1, directed by Shinichiro Watanabe, *Anime News Network*, March 11, 2005, http://www. animenewsnetwork. com/review/samurai-champloo/dvd-1 (accessed June 5, 2007).
[2]Ibid.

world. "I believe that children's souls are the inheritors of historical memory from previous generations. As they grow older and experience the everyday world, that memory sinks lower and lower. I feel I need to make a film that reaches down to that level. If I could do that I would die happy," he says.[88]

The films of Miyazaki Hayao, such as Spirited Away *(2001), have become well known around the world.*

Notes

Introduction: Creating a Unique Culture

1. Dr. M. Lal Goel, "A Few Observations on Japanese Culture and Politics," revised version of speech delivered at Japan-America Society of Northwest Florida, August 24, 2000, http://64.233.169.104/search?q=cache: ff6ZZVe7rmMJ:www.uwf.edu/lgoel/ documents/AObservationson JapaneseCulturePol.pdf+Japan+ cultural+borrowers&hl=en&ct= clnk&cd=8&gl=us&client=safar (accessed July 20, 2007).

2. Ronald E. Dolan and Robert L. Worden, eds., *Japan: A Country Study*, 5th ed., Washington, D.C.: Federal Research Division, Library of Congress, 1992 (Library of Congress Call Number DS806 .J223 1992), http://lcweb2.loc.gov/cgi-bin/query/r?frd/cstdy:@field(DOCI D+jp0118) (accessed July 20, 2007). Also available in book form.

Chapter 1: The Decorative and Fine Arts

3. John Reeve, *Japanese Art in Detail* (Cambridge: Harvard University Press, 2005), 118.

4. "Netsuke," *Japanese Art and Architecture New Users System (JANNUS)*, http://www.aisf.or.jp/~jaanus/deta/n/netsuke.htm (accessed March 10, 2007).

5. "Mary Cassatt: Maternal Caress (16.2.5)," in *Timeline of Art History* (New York: The Metropolitan Museum of Art, 2000), http://www.metmuseum.org/toah/hd/prnt2/hod_16.2.5.htm (accessed March 18, 2007).

6. Kakuzo Okakura, *The Book of Tea*, http://www.gutenberg.org/dirs/etext 97/tboft11.txt (accessed March 10, 2007).

7. Robert Sandall, "At last, the witch hunt is over," *The Sunday Times*, February 25, 2007, http://entertainment. timesonline.co.uk/tol/arts_and_entertainment/music/article 1419 318.ece (accessed March 10, 2007).

8. Peter Frank, "Yoko Ono as an Artist," *ArtCommotion*, Issue 2, http://www.artcommotion.com/Issue2/VisualArts/ (accessed March 10, 2007).

9. Jeff Michael Hammond, "Yasumasa Morimura: Los Nuevos Caprichos," *Metropolis*, http://metropolis. co.jp/tokyo/585/art.asp (accessed March 10, 2007).

10. Ibid.

11. Kay Itoi, "Season of Passion," *Artnet*, December 19, 2006, http://www. artnet.com/magazineus/features/itoi/itoi12-6-06.asp (accessed March 10, 2007).

Chapter 2: Writing Modern Japan

12. The Nobel Foundation, "Yasunari Kawabata: The Nobel Prize in Literature 1968: Biography," © The Nobel Foundation, 1968, From *Nobel Lectures, Literature 1968–1980*, Editor-in-Charge Tore Frängsmyr, Editor Sture Allén, World Scientific Publishing Co., Singapore, 1993), http://nobelprize.org/nobel_prizes/ literature/laureates/1968/kawabata-bio.html (accessed July 9, 2007).

13. Anders Osterling, "Presentation Speech: The Nobel Prize in Literature 1968," From *Les Prix Nobel en 1968*, Editor Wilhelm Odelberg, [Nobel Foundation], Stockholm, 1969, http://nobelprize.org/nobel_prizes/literature/laureates/1968/press.html (accessed July 9, 2007).

14. Yasunari Kawabata, "Japan, the Beautiful and Myself" (Nobel Lecture, December 12, 1968), © The Nobel Foundation, 1968, From *Nobel Lectures, Literature 1968–1980*, Editor-in-Charge Tore Frängsmyr, Editor Sture Allén, World Scientific Publishing Co., Singapore, 1993, http://nobelprize.org/nobel_prizes/literature/laureates/1968/kawabata-lecture-e.html (accessed July 9, 2007).

15. Ibid.

16. Ronny Green, "Buddhist Imagery in Snow Country," review and analysis of *Snow Country*, by Kawabata Yasunari, http://www. ronnygreen.us/Snow_Country.htm (accessed July 20, 2007).

17. The Nobel Foundation, "Kenzaburo Oe: The Nobel Prize in Literature 1994: Biography," © The Nobel Foundation, 1994, From *Les Prix Nobel. The Nobel Prizes 1994*, Editor Tore Frängsmyr, [Nobel Foundation], Stockholm, 1995, http:// nobelprize.org/nobel_prizes/literature/laureates/1994/oe-bio.html (accessed July 9, 2007).

18. Ibid.

19. Ibid.

20. Raicho Hiratsuka, *In the Beginning, Woman Was the Sun: The Autobiography of a Japanese Feminist* (quoted in Introduction), trans. Teruko Craig (New York: Columbia University Press, 2006), http://www.columbia.edu/cu/cup/publicity/raichoexcerpt.html (accessed July 8, 2007).

21. *Asiaweek*, "Fruits of Her Labor: A writer with Nobel ambitions," May 9, 1997, http://www.pathfinder. com/asiaweek/97/0509/feat2a.html (accessed July 10, 2007).

22. Celeste Heiter, review of *Kitchen*, by Banana Yoshimoto, trans. Megan Backus, *ThingsAsian*, January 6, 2002, http://www. thingsasian.com/stories-photos/1798 (accessed July 10, 2007).

Chapter 3: The Art of Japanese Architecture

23. Quoted in *Encyclopedia of World Biography*, s.v. "Kenzo Tange," http://www.bookrags.com/Kenzo_Tange (accessed June 20, 2007).

24. Quoted in "Kenzo Tange, Pritzker Architecture Prize Laureate, 1987," http://www.pritzkerprize.com/tange.htm (accessed July 29, 2007).

25. Ibid.

26. Ibid.

27. Ibid.

28. Quoted in "Architect Kenzo Tange," *Great Buildings Online*, http://www.greatbuildings.com/architects/Kenzo_Tange.html (accessed July 29, 2007).

29. Roland Berg, "Mr. Metabolism," *signandsight.com*, October 5, 2005, http://www.signandsight.com/features/392.html (accessed July 30, 2007).

30. Kurokawa Kisho, "Why the Philosophy of Symbiosis?" in *Each One a Hero: The Philosophy of Symbiosis*, http://www.kisho.co.jp/page.php/297 (accessed July 30, 2007). Also available in book form.

31. Belinda Luscombe, "He Builds With a Really Tough Material: Paper," *Innovators: Time 100: The Next Wave—Architecture and Design*, http://www.time.com/time/innovators/design/profile_ban.html (accessed July 30, 2007).

32. Ibid.

33. Peter Siegenthaler, "*Bunka-zai no Minshu-ka*: Folk Houses and the Democratization of Culture in Early Postwar Japan" (paper presented at Association for Asian Studies Annual Meeting, Japan Session 10, Chicago, IL, March 31–April 3, 2005), http://www.aasianst.org/absts/2005abst/Japan/j-10.htm (accessed June 20, 2007).

34. Mike Meyer, "Bound for Glory," *TIME.com*, August 30, 1994, http://www.time.com/time/magazine/article/0,9171,689508,00.html (accessed June 20, 2007).

35. Suzuki Hiroyuki, "Trees, Wind, Light, and Sound," *Process Architecture, Kansai International Airport Passenger Terminal Building* (Tokyo: Process Architecture Ltd., 1994), 15.

36. Ibid., 17.

37. Ibid., 19.

38. "Of Monuments, Machines, and Temporality," *Process Architecture, Kansai International Airport Passenger Terminal Building* (Tokyo: Process Architecture Ltd., 1994), 8.

39. Ibid.

40. Thomas Fisher, "The New Atlantis," *Process Architecture, Kansai International Airport Passenger Terminal Building* (Tokyo: Process Architecture Ltd., 1994), 31.

41. "Of Monuments, Machines, and Temporality," *Process Architecture*, 9.

42. Suzuki, *Process Architecture*, 15.

Chapter 4: The Performing Arts in Japan

43. "Takarazuka," *Japan Zone*, http://

www.japan-zone.com/modern/ takarazuka.shtml (accessed July 15, 2007).

44. Ibid.

45. Paul Binnie, "Japanese Noh Theater," *artelino—Art Auctions*, http://www. artelino.com/articles/noh_theater.asp (accessed July 20, 2007).

46. Ibid.

47. Iwasaki Mineko with Rande Brown, *Geisha, A Life* (New York: Washington Square Press, 2002), 1.

48. "Iki," *Japanese Architecture and Art Net Users System* (JAANUS), http:// www.aisf.or.jp/~jaanus/deta/i/iki. htm (accessed July 20, 2007).

49. Iwasaki, *Geisha, A Life*, np.

50. Ibid.

51. E. Taylor Atkins, *Blue Nippon: Authenticating Jazz in Japan* (Durham, NC: Duke University Press, 2001), back cover.

52. Atkins, *Blue Nippon*, 3.

53. Wakao Ailo, "Japan jazz fans bid sad farewell to historic café," *Washingtonpost.com*, January 27, 2007, http:// www.washingtonpost.com/wp-dyn/content/article/2007/01/27/AR2 007012701603.html (accessed July 15, 2007).

54. Atkins, *Blue Nippon*, 149.

55. Ibid., 191.

56. Ibid., 2.

57. Ian Condry, *Japanese Hip-Hop*, http:// web.mit.edu/condry/www/jhh/# story (accessed July 15, 2007).

58. Ibid.

59. Ibid.

60. Stephanie Schorow, "Japanese hip-hop: from 50 Cent to mirror balls and world peace," News Office, *Massachusetts Institute of Technology*, March 7, 2007, http://web.mit. edu/ newsoffice/2007/arts-japan-0307.html (accessed July 15, 2007).

61. Ibid.

Chapter 5: Japanese Cinema

62. Joseph L. Anderson and Donald Richie, *The Japanese Film: Art and Industry* (Princeton, NJ: Princeton University Press, 1982), 15.

63. Anderson and Richie, *The Japanese Film*, 14.

64. Ibid., 346.

65. Ibid., 103.

66. Ibid.

67. Donald Richie, *A Hundred Years of Japanese Film* (New York: Kodansha International, 2005), 82.

68. Anderson and Richie, *The Japanese Film*, 354.

69. Ibid.

70. Quoted in Nick Wrigley, "Ozu's Style," *Masters of Cinema: a Yasujiro Ozu resource*, http://www.ozuyasujiro. com/style.htm (accessed June 2, 2007). Adapted from a longer piece at *Senses of Cinema*.

71. Anderson and Richie, *The Japanese Film*, 359.

72. Ibid., 360.

73. Ibid., 362.

74. Ibid., 376.

75. Ibid., 380.

76. Quoted in Henrik Sylow, "Biogra-

phy," *kitano takeshi.com,* http://www.kitanotakeshi.com/index.php?content= biography (accessed June 2, 2007).

77. Quoted in Joan Dupont, "Actor, director, character, doppelgänger," *International Herald Tribune,* September 2, 2005, http://www.iht. com/articles/2005/09/01/opinion/dupont.php (accessed June 2, 2007).

78. Stefan Lovgren, "Horror, Japanese Style: Beyond 'The Grudge,'" *National Geographic News,* October 29, 2004, http://news.nationalgeographic.com/news/2004/10/1029_041029_th egrudge.html (accessed June 2, 2007).

79. Ibid.

80. Ibid.

81. Quoted in Ibid.

82. Michael Arnold, "Japanese Anime and the Animated Cartoon," *Midnight Eye,* November 29, 2004, http://www.midnighteye.com/features/animated_cartoon.shtml (accessed June 2, 2007).

83. Ibid.

84. Ibid.

85. Susan Napier, *Anime: Experiencing Contemporary Japanese Animation* (New York: Palgrave, 2000), 12.

86. Napier, *Anime,* 251.

87. Quoted in A. O. Scott, "Where the Wild Things Are: The Miyazaki Menagerie," *The New York Times,* June 12, 2005, http://www.nytimes.com/2005/06/12/movies/12scot.html ?ei=5088&en=ae85cb0218924e46&ex=1276228800&partner=rssnyt&emc=rss&pagewanted=all (accessed June 5, 2007).

88. Quoted in Xan Brooks, "A god among animators," *The Guardian,* September 14, 2005, http://film. guardian.co.uk/interview/interviewpages/0,6737, 1569689,00.html (accessed June 5, 2007).

For Further Reading

Books

Julia Altmann and Christopher Wynne. *One Day in Japan with Hokusai*. New York: Prestel Publishing, 2001. Altmann and Wynne use Hokusai's woodblock prints to tell the story of two children going to Tokyo to visit their grandfather.

Megumi Biddle and Steve Biddle. *Origami: Inspired by Japanese Prints from the Metropolitan Museum of Art*. New York: Viking Juvenile, 1998. The Biddles are origami experts who use reproductions of woodblock prints as inspiration for this book of origami lessons. The book includes historical information about each print.

Patricia Donegan. *Haiku: Asian Arts and Crafts for Creative Kids*. North Clarendon, VT: Tuttle Publishing, 2004. This book introduces five styles of haiku and includes exercises and projects that walk readers through composing their own Japanese poetry.

Carol Finley. *Art of Japan: Wood-Block Color Prints*. Minneapolis: Lerner Publishing Group, 1998. Finley introduces readers to the world of Japanese *ukiyo-e* prints, including how they were made and the world they represented. She discusses the lives of woodblock artists and the use of Japanese prints by European artists.

Bobbie Kalman. *Japan—the culture*. New York: Crabtree Publishing Company, 2000. Part of Crabtree Publishing's Lands, Peoples, and Cultures series, this book introduces readers to Japan's fine arts, the Japanese people's love of nature, and other aspects of Japanese culture.

Roland Kelts. *Japanamerica: How Japanese Pop Culture Has Invaded the U.S.* New York: Palgrave Macmillan, 2006. Focusing on the forms of anime and manga, Kelts examines why Japanese art and culture have become so popular in the United States. In doing so, he discusses why these art forms are uniquely Japanese and why artists in the United States could never have invented them on their own.

Kamini Khanduri. *Japanese Art & Culture*. Chicago: Raintree, 2003. Khanduri's book provides background and examples of ten different types of Japanese art, including woodblock prints, folding screens, netsuke, and hand scrolls. The book covers cultural elements such as theater, architecture, gardening, and samurai armor as well.

Akira Kurosawa. *Something Like An Autobiography*. London: Vintage Books, 1983. Kurosawa's humble and sometimes humorous account of his life is an interesting read. He talks about moviemaking, his childhood, his family, and his life during World War II.

Teruyo Nogami. *Waiting on the Weather: Making Movies with Akira Kurosawa.* St. Paul, MN: Stone Bridge Press, 2006. Having spent fifty years as Akira Kurosawa's assistant, Nogami presents a unique perspective on the famous Japanese moviemaker and how many of his movies were made.

Scholastic, Inc. *Step-by-Step Manga.* New York: Scholastic, Inc., 2005. Five manga characters teach readers how to draw them, from stick figures to a variety of action poses.

Ruth Wells. *A to Zen: A Book of Japanese Culture.* New York: Simon & Schuster Children's Publishing, 1992. Wells uses the alphabet as a framework for explaining a wide range of topics in Japanese culture, from the martial art Aikido to the religion Zen Buddhism.

Kate T. Williamson. *A Year in Japan.* New York: Princeton Architectural Press, 2006. This book is a re-creation of the artist's journal that Williamson kept during her stay in Japan. Divided into theme-based topics, the book combines Williamson's watercolor illustrations with her firsthand impressions of daily life in Japan.

Internet

AsianInfo.org. "Japanese Architecture." http://www.asianinfo.org/asianinfo/japan/architecture.htm. This article provides an overview of Japanese architecture, as well as detailed information about Buddhist architecture, Shinto architecture, and modern Japanese architecture.

Discovery.com. "Tokyo's Sky City." *Discovery Channel Feature: Extreme Engineering—Larger than Life.* http://dsc.discovery.com/convergence/engineering/skycity/interactive/interactive.html. This virtual tour illustrates the ideas of a group of Japanese architects who hope to reduce overcrowding in cities by building a series of towers that would create a vertical city taller than the world's tallest skyscraper.

J-Music.com. http://www.j-music.com. This site is a collection of home pages for Japanese jazz and *hougaku* (traditional) musicians. Visitors can watch videos of musical performances as well.

Kids Web Japan. http://web-japan.org/kidsweb. This site, sponsored by Japan's Ministry of Foreign Affairs, provides a wide range of cultural experiences for children. They can read Japanese folk legends, learn Japanese words and phrases, explore Japanese pop culture, find recipes for traditional Japanese foods, and discover what kids in Japan do for fun.

Index

Picture Credits

Cover photo: Time & Life
   Pictures/Getty Images
AFP/Getty Images, 32, 37, 38, 40, 53,
   56, 57, 65, 69, 73, 75, 77, 78
DeA Picture Library/Getty Images, 17
Getty Images, 45, 49, 54, 70, 76
Hulton Archive/Getty Images, 16, 25,
   27, 30, 61, 68

Ozaki Kokusai/Bridgeman Art Library/
   Getty Images, 18
Time & Life Pictures/Getty Images, 14,
   20, 22
Utagawa Hiroshige/Bridgeman Art
   Library/Getty Images, 24

About the Author

Patty J. Ruland is an investigative reporter and children's author who lives in Austin, Texas. She has written for newspapers, magazines, and children's publishers. Titles in print include *All About You, All About Sports,* and *SeaBase Nautilus.* She holds a Master of Liberal Arts degree from St. Edward's University in Austin.

About the Consultant

Dr. Christopher Gerteis is an assistant professor of East Asian History at Creighton University in Omaha, Nebraska.

31901046102556